OUR GAME

OUR GAME

New Zealand Rugby at 150

RON PALENSKI

mower

A catalogue record for this book is available from the National Library of New Zealand

ISBN 978-1-988516-98-1

A Mower Book
Published in 2020 by Upstart Press Ltd
Level 6, BDO Tower, 19–21 Como St, Takapuna 0622
Auckland, New Zealand

Design by CVD Limited
Printed by Everbest Printing Co. Ltd., China

To those who first decided rugby would be
New Zealand's game . . . and those who passed it on.

INTRODUCTION

A couple of long manuka branches, one end sharpened and stuck in the ground; another branch serving as a crossbar, lashed to the uprights with strips of flax. Jerseys, coats placed carefully on the ground to mark the lines of touch. Sheep cleared out of the way.

In the towns, the gutters are the touchlines. A chalk line across the road serves as the goal-line. The local cop frowns at posts in the middle of the road so no goals. Only tries count. If cars approach, the move stops until they're gone then the move resumes.

At the city's big rugby ground, the groundsman is out at first light marking out the white lines, pushing what looks like a lawnmower with a paint pot on top. The scoreboard is made ready. The home team name, painted in white on black-painted plywood, goes up first. Then one that just says 'Visitors'. At some more sophisticated grounds, the actual team name is used.

In a hotel somewhere, players gather for lunch. They don't talk much; just eat and wait for the time the coach or the captain stands and tells them what's required of them that afternoon. The words are simple and straightforward but heartfelt. There's no St Crispin's Day speeches, no 'From this day to the ending of the world, but we in it shall be remembered'.

Players file into the sheds, putting bags down at their usual spots, then outside for a sniff of the air, a look at the ground, toss a bit of turf in the air to test the wind. Then back inside. The slow ritual of dressing for the arena. Some don their knight's armour in a specific order — right sock, left sock, jersey. Others don't bother. Some seek a rub from the masseur, who's probably the butcher during the week, others just slap a bit of oil of wintergreen on their legs themselves. For most, the boots go on last. They stamp down on the concrete, just to make sure all is well. If they have to wait, they jog up and down on the spot; when the whole team does it, it sends shivers down rugby spines.

The referee, clad all in white, pokes his head in the door. 'Okay, time to go,' he might say.

Out into the wintry sunlight. Out into the roar. Or perhaps just polite applause. The game is to begin. The game's the thing.

That's rugby. Times, fashions, attitudes and demands change, the boy who plays in the street could grow up to be the focus of all eyes on the international arena; those who play in the back paddock could one day find themselves at Twickenham or Murrayfield or any of the other great rugby venues around the world.

Rugby is New Zealand's game. It has been for at least 150 years, probably for a year or two longer. Other sports were first organised around the same time in New Zealand, a period when the reach of the railways and the telegraph made people more aware of what else was happening in their land. But no other developed quite like rugby, no other captured such a hold on a young country that it was never to be loosened.

You can pick a country's game when driving. You see the playing fields and you know what sports are played there. The soccer goalposts in most countries. The four upright posts in Australia that denote their unique game. Baseball diamonds in the United States. Rugby goalposts. You see them more in New Zealand; perhaps only Wales could match it.

Rugby also has a hidden element, a part that goes beyond the television and radio coverage, the acres that used to be in newspapers and which now gets spread around online. The hidden part is the knowledge that a great many New Zealanders have of the game and how they love getting together to learn more or to share their knowledge. There are grown-ups who take pride in being able to name every member of a touring side from their youth; there are others who can remember scores. Eras define their memories. Older people may talk nostalgically of 1956 or 1959 or the golden era of the 1960s; younger ones have their recall conditioned by the professional era, who talk proudly of having seen Jonah Lomu. Some people live in houses crammed with rugby memorabilia; others have rooms devoted to All Blacks players' jerseys they've bought.

New Zealand provincial government was abolished in 1876 but provincial parochialism continues to define rugby followers. There are those who recall great eras for their provincial teams and even more remember great players and are blinkered to the claims of others.

And it's not just a man's game. Never was. Mothers, sisters, girlfriends followed their males and followed their game; some more passionately than the men. Find the oldest photo of a rugby crowd and chances are there will be women in the crowd. Some clubs and provincial unions used to have special seating areas for women, so as to protect them from the rougher, rowdier elements. Young women probably played the game informally from the beginning; there certainly was an attempt to form a women's professional team in the nineteenth century, long before men had the same idea.

Rugby is a game of the people, unlike in some countries. Whether left wing or right, socialist or capitalist, labourer or lawyer, it's all the same to rugby. As a chief justice, Sir Richard Wild, said when speaking at the seventy-fifth anniversary of the New Zealand union, 'There's no yielding to status in a rugby tackle, there's no privilege in a scrum.'

To many New Zealanders, the much-quoted words of John Mulgan still ring true: 'Rugby football was the best of all our pleasures.'

What follows are 150 stories on aspects of New Zealand rugby; if there's a heavy emphasis on the All Blacks, that's because the country emphasises the All Blacks. They are the pinnacle. They are the apex of the pyramid whose base is all New Zealanders.

FIRST GAME

A small advertisement appeared in the *Wanganui Herald* on 2 June 1869: 'Foot-Ball Match', it said. 'Country v Town. Town accepts the Country's Challenge, provided the Rugby Rules are attended to. Game to commence at 2 o'clock pm on Saturday, 12th inst. 2 June 1869.'

It's the first known indication of rugby being played in New Zealand. The game was postponed from 12 June and eventually took place the following week, with both the *Herald* and its tri-weekly contemporary, the *Chronicle*, reporting on it (and others later in the year).

The *Herald*, the paper founded by later prime minister John Ballance, reported: 'a football match was going on between fifteen of the town and same number of the country. The match was very well contested and after two hours hard kicking was withdrawn, rain and darkness coming on. The match will be resumed on Saturday week.'

FOOT-BALL MATCH.

" COUNTRY v. TOWN."—Town accepts the Country's Challenge, provided the Rugby Rules are attended-to. Game to commence at 2 o'clock p.m. on Saturday, 12th ins.

June 2, 1869.

Primary evidence from the Wanganui Herald.

Wanganui Chronicle

and

TURAKINA & RANGITIKEI MESSENGER.

TUESDAY, 22ND JUNE, 1869.

In order to make room for other important news, we have omitted one or two leading articles.

MASONIC BALL.--Thursday evening next is the date which is intended to be solemnized by high revelry. The United Free and Accepted Masons of Wanganui then intend to celebrate St John's Day by a Ball, at which they and their friends will do honour to the Patron Saint of Scottish Masonry.

SPORTS AT ARAMOHO.—The foot-ball match on Saturday was not terminated when night-fall brought the game to a termination. The country side, however, seemed to have the best of it, having had the ball in the neighbourhood of their goal for some considerable time, but were unable to kick it over the horizontal bar. The match is thus postponed for a fortnight. The trotting match resulted in the victory of Mr Higgie's mare. The running match did not come off as both the competitors were disabled in the foot-ball match.

The proof was in the playing.

It was clear rugby rules were 'attended to', as the advertisement wanted, by the *Chronicle*'s report: 'The foot-ball match on Saturday was not terminated when night-fall brought the game to a termination. The country side, however, seemed to have the best of it, having had the ball in the neighbourhood of their goal for some considerable time, but were unable to kick it over the horizontal bar. The match is thus postponed for a fortnight.'

Other references indicated rugby rather than one of the other football versions common for the time. In one game, the Country boys 'had the advantage in weight, which was counterbalanced by the pluck and splendid play of the Town boys'.

This undermines the orthodoxy that the first game of rugby in New Zealand was played in Nelson in 1870. Here was clear evidence that Wanganui was there first. Nelson had the advantage of its local paper listing the players involved in its first game in 1870, and these were later reproduced in Arthur Swan's *History of New Zealand Rugby Football*. Swan said the first game in Wanganui was in 1872, three years later. But further evidence of Wanganui's rugby primacy came from Tom Eyton, the part-promoter and advance man for the Natives' odyssey of 1888–89. He wrote in his account of that tour that he had played in a match, Armed Constabulary against Wanganui, in 1871.

There were also reports of Irish regiments of the British Army stationed in

12

New Zealand during the 1860s playing 'football', but there was no indication of which version. The 18th Regiment of Foot was said to have played a game in Wellington in 1868 but by which rules was not specified; the 18th was also stationed in Wanganui and was the last British regiment in New Zealand.

MONRO DOCTRINE

Charles John Monro introduced rugby to Nelson in 1870, no question. But whether his innovative act was the first game in New Zealand, or whether the game spread outwards from Nelson, is open to considerable question.

As we've seen, there is evidence of a game in Wanganui in 1869; there is no evidence that what happened in Nelson influenced footballers in places such as Auckland, Christchurch and Dunedin to adopt rugby rules.

Towns then were dots on a map not always connected; railways were in their infancy, overland travel otherwise was by foot, horse or horse-drawn coach; the super-highway of the day, the telegraph, was still developing. Most travel was by ship and letters from, say, Auckland to Christchurch often went via Sydney, Melbourne or Hobart. New Zealand in the 1860s and 70s was a frontier society. While there were newspapers in most places, they were largely confined to their own areas reporting their own news or what they could clip from papers brought by ship.

Monro came back from Christ's College in North London and told the young men of Nelson about the version of football played according to rules evolved at Rugby School. Hitherto they, like boys elsewhere in New Zealand, played different versions of football — some played Association (soccer), some Australian rules, some the rules of other English public schools. Some games were a mixture of rules; for example, half one version and half another.

The first game of rugby in Nelson was between Nelson College Old Boys and 'Town' and was played at the Nelson Botanical Reserve on 14 May 1870. A team of Nelson boys went to Wellington later in the year and played there too.

In 1904, a week after the All Blacks' first test in New Zealand, Monro recalled the Wellington venture: 'How we did enjoy ourselves, both victors and vanquished, and how little we thought in those remote times that football would one day become the great national game of the colony or that . . . some of us would form part of that vast multitude who on Saturday last cheered themselves hoarse when a crack team from England was so signally defeated by our successors and fellow countrymen.'

1875 AND ALL THAT

William Wills Robinson, more often published as W.W. Robinson, and known to some as 'Captain Billy', deserves more credit in the development of rugby in New Zealand than he generally receives. Generally, he receives none.

But Robinson was of profound influence in the 1870s when rugby gained precedence over various forms of football in the Auckland area. By Robinson's own account, he drafted rugby rules from memory in 1871, supplementing his memory with an 1865 *Lillywhite's Guide*. Teams in Auckland and Thames gradually took on rugby.

An Auckland cricket team (which Robinson captained) toured New Zealand in 1873 and he and leading rugby players decided rugby should follow suit, and they did so in 1875. Their first game was against Otago and this is generally acknowledged as the first interprovincial match.

Its greater significance was that the main football clubs in Dunedin, Dunedin and Union, which hitherto had played Association or Victorian rules, switched to rugby so they could give Auckland a game. They never switched back. The Aucklanders also played Christchurch Football Club, which had switched to rugby rules earlier in 1875 so they could play South Canterbury, who were captained by Alfred Hamersley, who had played four times for England, once as captain. A year later, Canterbury went north and played Auckland, also captained by Robinson, for the first time.

Robinson's role is at odds with the view that rugby radiated out from

Nelson. Given the poor communication of the time, it seems probable that like-minded people organised rugby wherever they were, heedless or ignorant of what had happened in Wanganui in 1869 or Nelson in 1870.

Robinson's actions, according to his own words, bear that out. But it was also a theory favoured by an early Wellington player and lawyer with a history bent, Edmund Bunny. 'In my opinion,' he wrote, 'there is no one who can claim to have been the father of rugby football in New Zealand. Each district in New Zealand developed its own organisation and no doubt there were one or two especially active players who were responsible for the origin and development of the game in each district.'

Robinson wrote a book, *Rugby Football in New Zealand — Its Development from Small Beginnings*, in 1905 based on articles he had written in the *Pall Mall Gazette*. Robinson, who was born in Birmingham on 17 June 1847, died in Wellingborough, Northamptonshire, on 14 September 1929.

EARLY BLUE

The annual match between Oxford and Cambridge universities, usually known just as the Varsity Match, is a British sporting institution with a status not much below that of the Boat Race. New Zealanders have been frequent players, with Chris Laidlaw captaining Oxford and the Blaikie brothers, John and Duncan, who both played for the Highlanders, captaining Cambridge.

New Zealand also had influence in the earliest days. Before the Varsity Match in 1929, a writer in *The Times* looked back on the 1875 match as one of great significance: it was the first time teams were fifteen-a-side (leading to internationals following suit), it was the first time that a goal was not required to win a match (just tries would do), and it was the last time Cambridge played in pink (their blue came the following year). The paper also noted that the 1875 game featured an Australian for the first time, contrary to an ingrained belief that Charles Gregory Wade became the first Australian in 1890 (he was Greg in his playing days and when he became a politician back home, he was Charles). *The Times* was sort of right.

The man in question was James Allen, who was born in Adelaide, but his mother died soon after his birth and father James took him to New Zealand. Young James also played in the Varsity Match in 1876. He had two spells of education in England, at St John's Cambridge and later at the School of Mines, but otherwise he was in New Zealand. He captained Otago in 1882 in the two games he played for the province (the second of which was against New South Wales, the first overseas visitors). He was later president of the Otago union (and presided when Pat Keogh, one of the great nineteenth-century players, was banned for betting on a match in which he played).

Allen became a Member of Parliament and was defence minister during the First World War and frequently acting prime minister when William Massey was on lengthy visits to London or the peace conference in Paris. Allen was in effect New Zealand's wartime leader. He was knighted in 1917. He became high commissioner to the United Kingdom in 1920 and was often with the 1924 All Blacks when they toured Britain and Ireland. He was part of the official entourage when royalty were introduced to the All Blacks and he presided at the end-of-tour functions at which two loving cups were presented.

FOOTY TO THE RESCUE

When Canterbury went south to Dunedin to play Otago in 1878, the players probably expected that travelling on the newly laid railway line was novelty enough.

But it became a footy trip to remember when they stopped in Timaru on the way back and could see drama unfolding out at sea. About an hour or so earlier, a fierce squall had whipped up the waves and five vessels anchored offshore were being tossed about.

When the players' train hissed to a stop, they could see that a couple of the boats had parted from their anchor cables and one had already washed up on the beach. Crew were being thrown around in the pounding surf.

As a story in the *Timaru Herald* said, 'now came the time for those on shore to show the stuff they were made of'.

Several of the players plunged into the raging waters and among them was William Varnham Millton, a promising young lawyer who was to become the founding treasurer of the Canterbury Rugby Union and who also played cricket for Canterbury. His teammates called him 'Scruffy', a nickname from his days at Christ's College.

A later report said of him: 'The dauntless fashion in which he plunged again and again into the boiling surf full of broken spars and wreckage to save life was not more marked than the perfect silence which he afterwards kept of his share in the day's events.'

Just under six years later, the silent hero Millton captained the first New Zealand

William Varnham Millton

team, one that was chosen by the Otago, Canterbury, Wellington and Auckland unions and which toured Australia as a reciprocal visit for the first by New South Wales two years before.

This team gained retrospective status as the first All Blacks — though their jersey was blue with a gold fernleaf — and survivors were given caps by the New Zealand union in the 1920s.

Millton was not among them. He died of typhoid three years after the tour, aged twenty-nine. (By a cruel coincidence, the captain of the first New South Wales team to visit New Zealand, Ted Raper, also died of typhoid, and didn't live to see the first New Zealand team in Australia.)

William Millton's younger brother, Edward Bowler Millton, was also in the 1884 team. When he died in 1942, his estate was left to the Sunlight League 'for the health, education and welfare of Canterbury children'. The E.B. Millton Charitable Trust still exists.

LONGEST TOUR

It was rugby's longest tour. By the time the New Zealand Natives got to Auckland for their last match in August 1889, it was a case of last men standing.

Since June the previous year, in New Zealand, Australia and the United Kingdom, they'd played 119 matches, twelve of those in the unfamiliar Australian rules against some of Melbourne's leading clubs.

For this exhausting odyssey, they had just twenty-six players and for many matches, because of injuries and fatigue, they had just the bare fifteen available. For some games, they couldn't even field fifteen. Along the way, local players were sometimes borrowed to make up the numbers.

This incredible tour was conceived and in large part organised by Joe Warbrick, an outstanding player of the period who had made his debut for Auckland when just fifteen. His original idea had been to choose a Maori side to play the visiting British team, the first from beyond Australia to tour New Zealand.

But that didn't prove possible for unstated reasons, most likely financial, so Warbrick extended his horizon and thought if they couldn't play the British in New Zealand, they'd have a go at them over there.

With the assistance of Tom Eyton, a Taranaki man who had played football with the Armed Constabulary, he set about organising a tour, the like of which rugby had not seen before and has not seen since. He also enlisted the help of a Gisborne publican, Jimmy Scott.

In one of the early games, against Auckland, Warbrick broke an ankle and, already worried about playing strength, decided to enlist some non-Maori. He adroitly changed the name to New Zealand Natives in the belief all players were native-born, that is, born in New Zealand. That wasn't so, but they became and remained the Natives.

Some of the Natives were of the highest quality: Tom Ellison, one of the great thinkers of the game in the nineteenth century; Dick Taiaroa, brother of Jack who'd played for the 1884 New Zealand team; Davy Gage was something

Frank Marshall – Football – The Rugby Game

The New Zealand Natives of 1888–89 . . . the longest tour.

of a Billy Wallace of his day, popping up in various positions; Pat Keogh, one of the ring-ins, was years later described as the best back in New Zealand in his time. Warbrick had four brothers or half-brothers with him on tour, and three Wynyard brothers were also in the squad.

Once it was known they'd also be playing Australian rules games, they enlisted the assistance of a Melbourne coach, Jack Lawlor, whose contribution was more a drain on finances than an aid to performance.

The Natives set the tone for much of the touring to follow, as well as seeing their black jersey with the silver fernleaf become the official garb of the New Zealand union when it was formed three years after the tour.

LADIES FIRST

More than a century before rugby took the momentous step in 1995 of abandoning its amateur ethos, a small group of New Zealand women did the same thing. In 1891, when women's football was hardly considered, an

Oamaru-born Aucklander, Nita Webbe, placed advertisements in newspapers around the country calling for young women to take up the game. The idea was to form two teams and take them round the country and to Australia, playing each other in exhibition matches (and with the idea of inspiring yet more women to take up the game).

She planned to pay her players 10 shillings a week (about $85 today). According to the *Auckland Star*, Webbe had thirty women in training and they 'have already obtained a fair degree of proficiency in manipulating the leather'. But the newspaper's editorial writer thought women were 'constitutionally unfitted' for rugby and such games would be 'essentially unwomanly'.

Webbe wrote to the paper, pointing out the increasing areas open to women (and, in two years, women in New Zealand would become the first in the world to have the right to vote). 'Strict observance to the rules will be enforced and when they play in public I am confident that the verdict will be not only that there has not been the slightest breach of propriety, but that a cleverer game has seldom been seen here,' Webbe insisted.

But it was not to be.

About a month later, newspapers reported the scheme had been abandoned and the weekly *Observer* recorded, without further explanation, 'a certain action for damages having broken down, the projected team of female footballers has come to nought'. That led to an assumption that neither Webbe nor her husband, Frederick Cleaver Webbe, had the money to carry the idea through. As the men's game would discover in the 1970s and 80s, promises of payment in the game were difficult to back up with delivery.

So the embryonic women players trained but didn't play.

Women or girls would undoubtedly have joined in games at picnics or fairs, but the first known game involving only women was at Newtown Park in Wellington in 1915. The women played at halftime of a men's match in a day of sport on 12 June 1915 to raise money for the Wounded Sailors' and Soldiers' Fund. Though the game was necessarily brief, it was rugby. The referee, May du Chateau, was a daughter of one All Black, Harry Roberts, and the sister of another, Teddy Roberts. 'After much excitement,' the *Evening Post* remarked, 'the match ended in a draw, each side scoring an unconverted try.'

A UNION FORMED

A Yorkshireman, a Lowland Scot and a Highland Scot, an Irishman from Cork, an Aucklander whose family came from Londonderry and County Mayo, and three other native-born colonials sat around a table at the Club Hotel in central Wellington on a Saturday night, 16 April 1892. Each of them became a midwife to the birth of the New Zealand Rugby Football Union.

They had been urged to attend by Denny Hoben, a red-haired Aucklander of Irish extraction, a journalist whose burning ambition was to form a national rugby union. He'd lived in Hawke's Bay and Wellington, had managed the Hawke's Bay team, was friends with many players, and knew the difficulties of organising rugby without a national body. He moved the motion that the NZRFU be formed and an Auckland-born saddler, Henry Joseph Haliday, seconded.

The other two native-born colonials, George Campbell, a government auditor, and Tom Newth, a Manawatu carpenter who played in the local brass band, were in favour. So too was Barney Ronaldson, a public trustee who had been born in Cork, and the Yorkshireman, dentist Bert Ginders.

But the two Scots, William Deans Milne born in Ontario of Aberdeenshire parents, and Thomas Smith Marshall, the Canterbury union secretary who had been born in Greenock, said no. The ayes had it. Letters of support had been received from Nelson, Wanganui and Marlborough unions.

The union was formed without Canterbury, Otago and Southland (they joined three years later). Essentially, the southern unions did not like the idea of being ruled from Wellington. Milne, a promising lawyer, said a national union would undermine the self-government of the provincial unions.

The eight men who made such a portentous decision for New Zealand rugby had an average age of twenty-seven, the oldest being Ronaldson, thirty-five, and the youngest, Ginders, who was just nineteen.

Hoben, who was a political and music writer for the *Evening Post* in Wellington, had toured the country the year before with his brother Sydney, a concert pianist, encouraging support for a national union. He became its founding (unpaid) secretary and for the next four years worked to get Otago, Canterbury and Southland to join, then tried unsuccessfully to form an Australasian union with New South Wales and Queensland. Hoben left in 1896 to take up a job on the weekly *Sydney Mail*; he worked back in New Zealand early in the twentieth century, then moved to Melbourne where he died in 1918.

ELLISON WALKABOUT

About seventy-five years before Keith Murdoch sought anonymity in the Australian hinterland, one of New Zealand rugby's leading men of the nineteenth century may have done the same.

Tom Ellison was an innovative thinker on and off the field: he was a member of the 1888–89 Natives on their two-hemisphere odyssey and, when home, he adapted a position he'd seen into the wing forward, which became a distinguishing feature of the New Zealand game until 1932. He was a Wellington delegate to the first annual meeting of the NZRFU and successfully moved that the Natives' jersey of black with a silver fern become the national team uniform and, fittingly, he captained the first team to wear it, in Australia in 1893.

Ellison after his playing days was a man of substance. He was a lawyer with chambers in central Wellington, seeking justice on ill-gotten Maori land his main specialty; he was a licensed native interpreter, as they were known, and he was owner of several properties. He was a Wellington rugby selector and played cricket in the summer; he was also a wrestler of some repute and a golfer. He was well liked and mixed in the Maori and Pakeha worlds with ease.

But in 1895 he was arrested and charged with procuring an abortion at the same time as a husband and wife were arrested for performing the illegal operations. The case dragged on for months; the chief abortionist was eventually convicted and jailed for eighteen years but they refused to implicate Ellison and the charge against him was dismissed.

A few months later, a paragraph appeared in a Hastings paper saying that Ellison was in Menzies in a remote area of Western Australia (about 700 km east of Perth) and had played a game there. The story gave no source, but it might have come from Ellison's cousin, Jack Taiaroa, the 1884 All Black who was a lawyer in Hastings. It was repeated, again without attribution, a few days later in the *Evening Post* in Wellington. On 19 June 1896, a newspaper in Perth reported that Ellison was going to coach the Fremantle team. But he was back in Wellington later in the year because he stood unsuccessfully

Tom Ellison

for Parliament. His reputation was clearly not diminished because he was talked of as being manager of the 1905–06 New Zealand team, but he died the year before that tour. One of his obituaries recalled him as 'one of the finest exponents of football in Australasia — perhaps in the world'.

DEATH ROLL

A popular wing, Barney Armit, was paralysed as a result of a tackle in a match in Dunedin in August 1899. He lingered in hospital for about three months until he died, the first All Black to die as the result of injury in a game.

Two more were to follow.

Alexander McNaughton Armit, born at Inverkeithing in Scotland in 1874, played nine matches for New Zealand in Australia in 1897. The fatal tackle came two years later, on 26 August 1899, when he was playing for Otago

Barney Armit

Nicky Allen

against Taranaki. The tackler was Alf Bayly, who captained the All Blacks on Armit's one tour and who was later president of the New Zealand union.

Between the tackle and the death, there were various reports about what happened and Armit himself, paralysed from the neck down, said Bayly was not to blame. Two versions dominated at the inquest: one that Armit crashed to the ground while trying to hurdle Bayly; the other that Bayly upended Armit and dropped him. The coronial jury's verdict was: 'That deceased died from injury received in a football match, that the occurrence was purely accidental, and that no blame attaches to anyone.' Bayly was reported to have played just once more for Taranaki after the Otago game.

An Auckland forward, Bert Palmer, an All Black in 1928, 1929 and 1932, died from a head injury sustained in a club match in September 1932. He was playing for Otahuhu when he went down after his head hit the hip of a University player, Norman Jenkin. He was taken to a private hospital, then to Auckland Hospital where he underwent surgery. But he never regained consciousness. The All Blacks, Otahuhu and his former club Ponsonby were represented by pallbearers at his funeral. At the inquest a couple of days later, various players described the game as being normal and Jenkin said there was nothing unusual about Palmer's tackle. The coroner ruled Palmer died from a cerebral haemorrhage.

Fifty-two years later, in 1994, another popular All Black died as a result of injury. Nicky Allen, an All Black in 1980 described as a supernova by captain Graham Mourie, was playing in a club match at Port Kembla, a suburb of Wollongong in New South Wales, when he was tackled and fell back, his head hitting the ground. He had had a history of head injuries. Allen, in a coma, was taken to the city hospital where he died.

FOREIGN COACH

The concept of a foreign coach is a relatively modern one, rugby following soccer's lead — as it often has — by going beyond national borders for a coach. New Zealand and South Africa among leading countries haven't done it yet, but most countries have at some stage had coaches from somewhere else.

Many of the foreigners have been New Zealanders — Graham Henry and Steve Hansen with Wales, Warren Gatland with Ireland and Wales, and others of lesser profiles. Robbie Deans goes on the list for having coached Australia from 2008 until 2013 and frequently is referred to as the Wallabies' first foreign coach.

But no. The first time an Australian team took the field, in 1899, the coach was a New Zealander.

William Warbrick was the second youngest of the five brothers/stepbrothers who went on the long 1888–89 Natives' tour, and who later played for both Queensland and New South Wales. He was a boatbuilder and prominent in football in Sydney when Matthew Mullineux led his British team to Australia in 1899. When the first Australian test team was named, the *Sydney Morning Herald* said it would be training that afternoon and 'Mr W Warbrick will supervise the work'.

So he was a coach by function if not by name. Not only did he coach the first Australians, he was also a touch judge in the first match (the other was Blair Swannell, who played for both Great Britain and Australia). And just to complete the unusual facts of that first test, the referee was also a New Zealander, William ('Gun') Garrard from Christchurch, who thus became the first southern hemisphere neutral referee.

Jim Gleeson, a member of the first New Zealand league team in 1907 and its de facto manager, recalled in the 1930s the influence Billy Warbrick had had. Warbrick, he wrote, used to frequently call into the central Sydney office of the weekly sports paper, the *Referee*, and talk over games of the past and the future. 'What a knowledge of rugby Billy Warbrick had,' Gleeson wrote. 'It was an education in the scientific side of the game and a rare privilege to listen to his dissertation on how games had been lost and won and how they would be fought out a few days' hence. He was one of the generals of rugby.'

Warbrick didn't live long to enjoy his newfound status as Australian coach. He developed consumption (tuberculosis) and returned home to die, settling back on family land in Bay of Plenty only a few weeks before his death on 28 October 1901, aged thirty-five. Four of the Warbrick boys died young — he was first, followed by Arthur, who drowned in 1902; then Joe, killed by a geyser in 1903; then Frederick, also of consumption, who died in 1904.

A FRACTIONAL CHANGE

Ever wonder why New Zealand rugby has first and second five-eighths and the rest of the world doesn't?

The answer, as with many quirks of the game, resides in the nineteenth century during rugby's formative years. It apparently happened after an annual match between the Dunedin club, Alhambra, and Merivale of Christchurch in 1891. Jim Baker, an Alhambra and Otago forward, recorded that Jim McCleary, a noted rugby tactician of the day, introduced the new position, though it was given its name by Baker.

McCleary, the father of 1924 All Black Brian McCleary, wanted to try a new experiment in the Alhambra backs to confuse Merivale. He told Billy Johnston, a well-known Otago footballer and cricketer, to move out of the scrum when Alhambra were inside the Merivale twenty-five, and to make himself as useful as he could among the backs.

After the game, won by Alhambra, one of the Merivale men asked: 'Where did that extra man come from? He wasn't a halfback and he wasn't a three-quarter.'

To which Baker replied: 'If he's not a halfback and not a three-quarter, then he must be a five-eighth.'

The name — and the tactic — stuck and soon other provinces adopted what they saw as a winning advantage, and island and national teams followed suit.

As much as World Rugby, the former International Rugby Board, has tried to bring uniformity into the game, especially since the end of the amateur era, it has failed to impose on the world one set of positional names. To most New Zealanders, a first five-eighth is precisely that (even if it's often misspelt 'five-eight'), but a second five-eighth often gets labelled as a second centre, which he's not, or the nebulous, imprecise 'midfield'. While we stick to ours, others stick to theirs: the position has more names than any other in rugby — flyhalf, standoff, outhalf, demi d'ouverture, quite apart from literal translations into any number of other languages.

Coaches and commentators in the modern game have tried to overcome this plethora by simply calling the player in the position 'the ten', just as they refer to halfbacks (or the scrumhalf) as 'the nine'. That's all very well in the modern jargon but could be confusing if used retrospectively. In the old numbering system, 'the ten' used to be 'the six' and 'the nine' used to be 'the seven'. And when tour numbers, usually derived from an alphabetical list of players, were worn, it was entirely likely for the first-five to be 'the twenty-two' or any other number between one and thirty.

THE FIRST TEST

A day worthy of noting on the international rugby calendar is 15 August, because it was on that day in 1903 that New Zealand played its first test, against Australia in Sydney. Previous matches had been intercolonial affairs against New South Wales and Queensland. (Australia became a nation and the separate colonies became states on 1 January 1901.)

This was the day New Zealand and Australia met for the first time in a test match. It was a 22–3 win for the All Blacks and people as long as their memories lasted recalled the 1903 side as being worthy to rank with the 1905 and 1924 teams.

The Australians began their test history with four matches against a Great Britain team in 1899, even though an Australian union was not formed until

The Great Rugby Football Match.

AUSTRALIA v. NEW ZEALAND.

BY WANDERER.

A new era—Australia v New Zealand at football—Australia, that is, Queensland and New South Wales, the two Australian States out of the six that play Rugby. The title is rather ambitious, perhaps, and possibly New South Wales and Queensland combined would have better suited the circumstances. Will we ever be able to put a genuine Australian team in the field, whether Rugby, Australian, or "Soccer?" I am sure never at Rugby, never against England at Australian, and apparently hopeless at British Association. Saturday was the first occasion in the history of football that Queensland and New South Wales have joined forces against New Zealand. It is, however, doubtful whether the combination resulted in a better side being pitted against the visitors than New South Wales single handed could have placed in the field. The methods of the two State teams are dissimilar, the combination had no practice together, therefore it was a combination in title only. Perhaps we would have seen more combination from a team of N.S.W. players. There was no unanimity of opinion as to how the Australian team would shape. But it was generally thought the New Zealanders were too good for any fifteen we could place in the field, though it was considered that the home side would play a harder game than any that had hitherto met the visitors, and that the margin of victory would be comparatively small. The contrary was the result. The combined fifteen fairly well held their opponents up to half time, but afterwards it was simply a succession of scores for New Zealand.

Most of us have observed that in all the matches played by the New Zealanders in Sydney, they do not appear to begin play until the second half, and then they run clean over every one who would block their progress. It matters not to them whether a pass be off side or whether there be a knock-on, they go right on, forgetting all about the existence of the referee until they hear the whistle sound. There is no deliberation about them at all. A system apparently without a thought. They think afterwards. With the Australians it is different. In the case of something occurring which is palpably illegal there is a momentary and frequently a fatal pause. If the whistle sounds it is all right, if it do not, then points follow to the visitors. This was painfully brought home to us on Saturday when we saw the Australian team "fising" out at the touch line while R. M'Gregor was running behind the home goal. M'Gregor went on until the whistle sounded, and then it was the acknowledgment that a try had been secured. That couple of seconds' deliberation by the home fifteen cost five points. The visitors play a game altogether different to the Australians. In their forward rushes they bump an opponent to the ground and walk over him or to the side, and so do some of them when running with the ball in possession. It is simply the survival of the fittest. Not brute strength has rather too much to do with the game. The New Zealanders are sufficiently clever in working the scrums, in catching, line and goal kicking, in beating the tackle with smart passes, and in toe work, to defeat Australia with a good margin, in a sportsmanlike game instead of depending so much upon a force which carries with it considerable, if unchecked, illegal interference. Everything was in favour of a brilliant game. There were fears on the Friday evening that rain would spoil the contest, indeed some fairly heavy showers fell in the city up to 11 o'clock, but, fortunately, the morning broke bright and cheerful, the ground was dry, and everything surrounding the scene looked lovely. A great crowd, there were over 30,000 present, assembled to witness the first contest of its kind, and among the interested spectators were his Excellency the Governor-General, Lord Tennyson, his Excellency the State Governor, Sir Harry Rawson, and parties from the respective Government Houses. Everything worked up to a great contest, and everyone expected a brilliant exhibition of Rugby. The game was a great one, as before mentioned, the visitors won easily, by 22 to 3, but

J. R. Henderson, Selector. S. Boland. A. Burdon. E. E. Larkin. F. C. Lea, Referee. L. Evans. P. Nicholson. D. Lutge. H. D. Wood, Selector.

J. E. Jones. H. A. Judd. S. Wickham, Captain. C. White. J. W. Maund.
C. Redwood. S. Riley. W. Hardcastle. A. Gralton.

AUSTRALIAN FOOTBALL TEAM, 1903.

COLLAPSE OF A "SCRUM."

Part of the Sydney Mail's coverage of the first test.

1949. For the single match in 1903, the Australians were selected by two from the New South Wales union (Harry Wood and Jim Henderson) and one from Queensland (Fred Lea) and played in the light blue jerseys of New South Wales.

One report had a crowd of 30,000 at the Sydney Cricket Ground to watch New Zealand have a decisive win, so decisive that it left some Australian reporters despairing about whether their country would ever be good enough. 'It seems almost impossible,' one said, 'for Australia to put a side into the field with any hope of victory.'

The test was part of an eleven-match tour, during which New Zealand lost only once — and that was in a shakedown match against Wellington before the All Blacks crossed the Tasman. One of the All Blacks forwards, George Nicholson, later said: 'The 1903 All Blacks that toured Australia — that's the best team I ever saw or played with . . .' (Nicholson was a member of the 1905–06 team in the northern hemisphere.)

The weekly *Sydney Mail* took a gloomy view after this historic encounter: 'It seems hopeless to expect to ever score a substantial victory over the Maorilanders,' it said. 'A suitable climate and a longer season have made New Zealand the headquarters of rugby in the southern hemisphere . . . we could, with, say, annual meetings look forward to considerable improvement in our method of playing rugby.' That improvement didn't take long. New Zealand and Australia drew one test in 1907 and the Wallabies beat the All Blacks for the first time in 1910.

The New Zealand captain in this first test was Jimmy Duncan, a five-eighth from Otago who was the only survivor of the previous tour, in 1897. He was later coach of the 1905–06 team in the United Kingdom, Ireland and France.

BILLY THE BRAVE

The Victoria Cross, the supreme award in the Commonwealth for acts of bravery in the face of the enemy, was awarded seventy-eight times during the Boer War between 1899 and 1902. One of them was to a New Zealand

Captain William Hardham in First World War uniform.

trooper, William James Hardham, who had rescued a wounded mate under fire. It was the first VC to go to a New Zealander.

Twelve New Zealanders were ordered to charge a kopje (small hill) where Boer fighters were holed up. Hardham rode about forty or fifty metres ahead of others in an advance guard and he happened to look around and notice that the horse of one of the other troopers, John McRae, had been shot from under him, leaving McRae on the ground and no chance of getting clear.

According to the citation in the *London Gazette*, Hardham 'at once went under a heavy fire to his assistance, dismounted and placed him on his own horse, and ran alongside until he was guided to a place of safety'. It was subsequently found that McRae's horse had twelve bullets in it.

Hardham was one of the soldiers singled out to make up the New Zealand contingent at the coronation parade for King Edward VII in 1902.

Billy Hardham (1876–1928) was widely known as a rugby player of such repute it seems surprising he was never an All Black, especially given some less than rigorous selection policies of the time. He played for Wellington between 1897 and 1908 and was later a Wellington administrator and was made a life member of the Wellington union.

He served again in the First World War and was twice invalided home. In Egypt in 1915 before the Gallipoli campaign, Hardham organised rugby. 'I tried hard for a long time to secure a rugby football,' he wrote home, 'but could not get one in Egypt. Some of the other regiments, however, had brought a few with them and I managed to borrow one.'

Hardham was given a civic welcome when he returned to Wellington in 1916 to recuperate from wounds sustained on Gallipoli. The Hardham Cup continues to be one of the trophies in Wellington club rugby.

Another rugby player, Henry Donald Coutts, who had played for Taranaki in the 1890s, won a Queen's Scarf, the next best thing in the Boer War to winning a VC. Queen Victoria personally knitted eight scarfs as special awards for bravery. Coutts was the only New Zealand recipient.

MYSTERY SECRETARY

Rugby is a player's game, but the administrators have always been pretty important too, whether in the earliest days or the latest. For the most part, they're out of the public eye and when they finish with rugby, they disappear from sight.

Take Alfred Mark de Costa, for example. He took over from the New Zealand union's founding secretary, Denny Hoben, in 1896 when Hoben moved to Sydney to further his journalistic career. De Costa was in office until 1901, which meant he organised inward and outward tours with New South Wales and dealt with any issues arising from players leaving to fight in the Boer War. But little has been published about him.

De Costa came from a London Jewish family that settled in Dunedin in the early 1860s then moved to Greymouth, following the gold strikes. Alfred Mark was born there and then went with the family to Gisborne. He moved to Wellington when he was in his mid-twenties and worked as a sharebroker and real estate agent while for five years he also fulfilled his voluntary duties with the NZRFU.

In 1907, in Christchurch, he met Ethel Benjamin, well known as being the first New Zealand woman law graduate and the second woman in the British Empire to be admitted to the bar. They married later in 1907 and not long after disappeared from New Zealand, leaving just the barest of traces.

Her family, which had settled in Dunedin, moved in its entirety back to Britain and she and Alf followed. They travelled on the continent for much of the between-wars years and bought a flat in Bordighera on the Italian Côte d'Azur, partly because Alf was a chronic asthma sufferer and it was thought the Mediterranean air would do him good. Bordighera was also popular in the late 1930s with Hitler's air chief, Hermann Goering, who was reported to have left there hurriedly when Germany took over Austria in 1939. Mussolini also made visits.

Bordighera was probably not the place to stay for a Jewish couple in wartime so they moved along the coast to Menton and, with other Jewish people, got away on a coal boat, apparently hiding at times in the hold.

Alf de Costa died a year after getting back to Britain, on 27 June 1941; his death certificate recording bronchitis and (chronic and acute) asthma as the causes of death. Ethel died two years later, on 14 October 1943, from a fractured skull sustained when she was hit by a 'motor utility brake' in London.

KILLED BY GEYSER

In a catalogue of unusual ways in which international rugby players met their deaths, Joe Warbrick's would rank as one of the strangest. Warbrick, one of half a team of sons of an English trader and a high-born Maori woman, helped shape rugby in New Zealand in the nineteenth century.

He played for Auckland when he was just fifteen, he was in the first New Zealand team in 1884 and he organised and led the Natives in 1888–89 on their world odyssey. This was the team that ushered in the black jersey and the silver fern.

One of Joe's brothers, Alf, was a noted guide in the North Island thermal region and in 1903, to fulfil a tourist's dare, he rowed a boat across the crater lake of the Waimangu Geyser. It was then at the height of its fame and unpredictable volatility and attracted tourists from home and overseas. Curious about his brother's feat, Joe rode from his farm about 60 km away to investigate.

He and some tourists walked down a lakeside path and Alf, sensing the geyser was about to blow, called for them to come back. Two Australian men who were nearer heard and returned but Joe, two sisters and an Auckland man carried on.

'We're all right, Mother,' one of the sisters cried out.

The geyser blew. Alf, the sisters' mother and other would-be rescuers raced down the path when the geyser's fury had subsided, but it was much too late. Joe's body was found 500 metres away, snagged on the branch of a tree. The bodies of the sisters and the Auckland man were nearby.

Alf Warbrick's boss in the newly established Department of Tourist and Health Resorts, Thomas Donne, cabled for an immediate report. Warbrick replied he could not write a report immediately because he was 'not altogether well enough'.

Joe Warbrick

Nevertheless, he and others there still wrote accounts of what they saw and appeared before an inquest in Rotorua the next day, which concluded that the four died from suffocation and burns, combined with shock, and no blame should be attached to Alf Warbrick because he had repeatedly warned people to stay away from the edge of the geyser.

Alf was the only one of the Warbrick footballers to reach old age; he died in 1940, aged about eighty.

GROUND ZERO

The All Blacks have played test matches at more than eighty grounds, some of them the great stadiums of the world, some of them perhaps not so great.

As well as the celebrated rugby venues such as Twickenham, the Millennium Stadium and Murrayfield, they've also played at Old Trafford, Wembley, Soldier

Field, the Melbourne Cricket Ground and, among others, Stadio Giuseppe Meazza which is better known as San Siro for the area of Milan where it is located.

And then there's Tahuna Park. That's the ground in Dunedin where New Zealand played their first home test, against Australia. It was in early September 1905 when Dave Gallaher's All Blacks were already on their way to Britain, so the team that played in Dunedin was in effect a Third XV.

They were supposed to have played at the Caledonian Ground in South Dunedin, where the British had played the year before, but several days' rain had left both it and the alternative venue, Carisbrook, waterlogged. On the morning of the game, the Otago and New Zealand unions were all for postponing it until the next day or the Monday. The Australian manager, Jim Henderson, and captain Stan Wickham said they wanted to start on the trip home on Monday and wondered about other options. So they hopped on a tram and went out to Tahuna Park which, being by the sea, was sand-based. It

Ron Palenski Collection

Tahuna Park, the venue for New Zealand's first home test against Australia.

was a bit wet, but they delayed the start until a quarter to four on the Saturday afternoon — hoping there'd still be enough daylight for its completion. The game went ahead without any problems and there was only an occasional shower during it. New Zealand won 14–3.

Tahuna Park, developed mostly as an agricultural showgrounds, was a regular venue for club rugby — and was to remain so for more than a century — as well as a variety of other sports, including harness racing and speedway. A league test against Great Britain was also played there in 1924.

Another unusual aspect to this test was that no programme appears to have been published, or none that avid programme collectors have ever seen. There appear to have been no photographs of the match, or none that appear in contemporary publications, and there was no photo of the New Zealand team. A studio photo of one of the All Blacks in the match, Hubert ('Jum') Turtill, dressed in an All Blacks jersey, popped up at auction in 2019, but on closer examination the photo was proven to have been taken by a studio photographer in St Helens, Merseyside, where Turtill later played league.

MEN IN BLACK

Rugby changed forever on 16 September 1905, the day the All Blacks first took the field in Britain. The match was against Devon in Exeter and New Zealand won 55–4, laying down a gauntlet to rugby in Great Britain and Ireland. The match showed to the British for the first time that there was rugby strength beyond their shores and that there were ways of playing the game that were different to theirs.

Sun-hatted Billy Wallace kicking goals was just one innovation. The Devon match also introduced the name 'All Blacks' to British newspaper readers; the name had been used every so often since the 1880s in New Zealand, but its use in Britain took it to a different level. It was first used in the Devon newspaper, the *Express and Echo*, in its Saturday night edition after the first game.

It wrote: 'The "All Blacks", as they are styled by reason of their sable and unrelieved costume, were under the guidance of their captain (Mr Gallaher).'

Despite that, there still arose a mistaken belief that rugby's best-known nickname came about through a reporter's hand. The myth, which sometimes still gets repeated despite ample evidence against and none for, was that the *Daily Mail* reporter, John Buttery, referred to the team as 'all backs' because of interpassing between forwards and backs but that someone in his office inserted an 'l'. Buttery was not in Devon for the first match; it was only after the result became known that most of Fleet Street thought the tour worth a closer look.

Billy Wallace himself helped the myth. He made a speech at a reunion of the team in Wellington in 1955 and said the name came about after the 63–0 defeat of West Hartlepool and it was in Buttery's coverage for the *Mail* that he referred to 'all backs'. But the evidence did not support him. Buttery's report went for fourteen paragraphs before it said: 'A glance at the undermentioned weights of the "all blacks" will convey some idea of the calibre of the team.'

NZ Rugby Museum

Sun-hatted Billy Wallace kicks for goal during the All Blacks' opening match in 1905.

Another erroneous version of the naming was that Buttery watched the team practice at Ealing in West London with one of the players, Ernie Booth. Buttery supposedly remarked that the players wore black belts, anklets and kneelets as well as shorts and jerseys.

'Oh, that's just to be all black,' Booth replied. When he died in 1935, one obituary perpetuated the myth.

LAND OF SONG

The pre-match rituals before a test match, part of what marketing people like to call the rugby experience, began by chance rather than design, a spur-of-the-moment decision.

It all stemmed from the 1905–06 New Zealand team's venture into the northern hemisphere. The All Blacks had performed their haka at concerts and receptions but only did it before a match for the first time at Blackheath, almost halfway through the tour.

There being no radio or television of course, British people could learn of the haka only from the newspapers or what they saw for themselves at the few matches at which it was done. The crowd at Crystal Palace, for example, before the England test was reported to have laughed so much the stand roof shook.

It wasn't a laughing matter in Wales. Before the Welsh test, the crowd had been singing that stirring song telling of Welsh resistance to English military might, 'Men of Harlech'. The last line, 'Cambria ne're can yield!' had just faded away when the modern gladiators strode into their coliseum.

The All Blacks formed themselves into a rough semi-circle and to the rhythmic slapping of thighs and thumping of boots on the turf, they chanted the best known of haka, 'Ka Mate!' The Welsh stood there and watched and when it was over, they looked at each other and began to sing:

Mae hen wlad fy nhadau yn annwyl i mi
Gwlad beirdd a chantorion, enwogion o fri

Although not as well known then as it is now, the crowd slowly joined in, sensing that the Welsh anthem may have been sung because the *Western Mail* had suggested it that morning as a counter to the haka.

The All Blacks were transfixed. Their vice-captain, Billy Stead, who was one of the touch judges that day, later wrote: 'A Welshman can be depended on to burst into song under the strain of any undue excitement and it must have thrilled every stranger as it did me to hear the populace, on the conclusion of our Maori war song, join in with their team and sing, in their dialect, their national anthem . . .'

The team manager, George Dixon, was just as enthused, talking about the 'whole, vast, swaying crowd, men and women alike, joining in. It was a wonderful sight and the air was electric with excitement.'

It's not often traditions have such a definitive beginning, but that was where the ritual of anthems before matches began. Only the order has changed, the haka now following the anthems, although there was a return to the original order when the centenary of the first match was marked in 2005.

BILLY THE BEST

You can talk of Billy Wallace or of Dave Gallaher, or the try-scoring Jimmy Hunter or Bill Cunningham and Charlie Seeling, the towering men of the forwards, but one man of the 1905–06 New Zealand team should be remembered ahead of them all: William John Stead.

Billy Stead was the vice-captain of the team and its tactical brain. It was he who, more than captain Gallaher or coach Jimmy Duncan, planned the defeat of every team they came across except for Wales. And it surely was no coincidence that Stead did not play on the always-recalled day in Cardiff.

Some said he was ill, some said he was injured; he said he stood down to give Simon Mynott a game, believing at that late stage of the tour Mynott was the fresher man.

Stead was also the chronicler of the tour. Words poured from his fluent pen. He wrote a weekly newspaper column that told where the All Blacks were and what factories or tourist spots they visited. They were a fascinating insight into a touring team at the start of the twentieth century.

And he wrote one of the classic rugby books. It was called *The Complete Rugby Footballer on the New Zealand System* and the cover proclaims it was written by Dave Gallaher and Stead. It is a remarkable book, made even more remarkable by the fact that Stead alone wrote it, in his words, in 'three days and four nights'.

Gallaher had been approached by a noted golf writer of the time, Henry Leach, to write a book about New Zealand rugby and its methods generally for a British

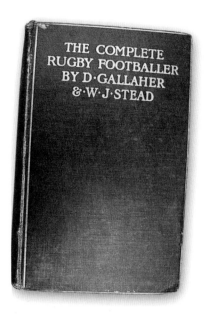

The gospel according to Billy Stead.

readership that was ignorant of the game beyond their own shores. Gallaher stayed with Leach after the Paris match in early 1906 and, realising the size of the task before them, enlisted Stead. Three typists were available but were not used because Stead had never dictated before so he sat down in Leach's house in Herne Hill and wrote the whole thing while Gallaher and Leach sorted out pictures and captions. George Tyler pitched in with some proofreading. Leach, according to Stead, was useless because he'd never seen a rugby match, but he completed the index and took the royalties.

Gallaher and Stead were each paid £50 and each distributed the money among their teammates, most of whom were broke at the end of the tour and living in lodgings in various parts of London while waiting on their ship to New York.

Stead's daughter Flo said her father also made most of the speeches required on tour, including one in French in Paris.

A MAN OF HIS TIME

Colin Gilray played once for New Zealand, against Australia in Dunedin in 1905 after the 'first' New Zealand team had left for Britain. Yet on the side of a house in Dundee, Scotland there is a plaque that says he was born there. Those two interconnected facts demonstrate an aspect of rugby that has all but disappeared.

Gilray, a wing for Otago, had been regarded as a certainty for the first tour of Britain but turned it down because of his university studies. His diligence was rewarded because he won a Rhodes Scholarship in 1907 and was able to continue his rugby career amid his Oxford obligations.

Gilray was at Oxford with Ronny Poulton, an England rugby favourite who, after he was killed in the war, *The Times* described as 'the greatest player of all time'. Gilray was certainly impressed by him. He wrote: 'I never left him even after a train journey from Paddington on a Saturday night . . . without feeling what a privilege it was to have been with him. Oxford was a greater and better experience because he was there.'

Colin Gilray

Since Gilray had been born in Dundee, he automatically qualified for Scotland and he played four times for the land of his birth between 1908 and 1912: two wins against England and losses to Ireland and Wales. He became the sixth to play test rugby for two different countries.

He went on to a remarkably influential and distinguished career. While studying for the bar in Britain, he taught at the exclusive rugby school in London, Mill Hill. He returned to New Zealand in 1913 and

40

worked as a lawyer in Milton, south of Dunedin, before he enlisted in the British Army and was commissioned in the Rifle Brigade; he survived the Somme, won a Military Cross and by the end of the war had a wife and an OBE as well.

He returned to the law in Otago but in 1922 became headmaster of a three-year-old Presbyterian-run school, John McGlashan College. Just over a decade later, he became the principal of Scotch College in Melbourne and according to biographer Geoffrey Serle, Gilray was 'a liberal humanist, kind despite the gruffness, modest and self-effacing'. He was twice deputy chancellor of the University of Melbourne and was involved in various groups geared to the advancement of secondary and tertiary education in Australia. He died in 1974, known more for his contribution to education than to rugby.

But he was not entirely forgotten. Someone in Dundee remembered the suburb Broughty Ferry produced an All Black, and a plaque was placed on the wall of the house where he was born and where he lived before his parents took him to Dunedin.

EVERYWHERE MAN

Ernie Booth was a complete rugby man of the early twentieth century: he played it as a fullback or centre, he coached it, he organised it, and he wrote about it. He played for New Zealand and for New South Wales, toured Britain as a journalist with the 1908 Wallabies (and played against them in 1909 for NSW), Britain in 1924 with New Zealand, and France and Britain in 1926 with the national Maori team.

During the First World War, Booth worked for the Australian YMCA in a welfare role which seemed to consist mainly of organising sports including of course rugby; he played in the odd match in France and refereed some. He played for Kaikorai and Otago at home, Newtown in Sydney and while in England, he played for Leicester. After the war, Booth was hired as coach

Ernie Booth

at £6 a week by the Southland union until someone read the rules on professionalism. The New Zealand union said taking the role made him a professional, but Booth took it anyway, and found some other way of earning money. His brief was to mould a Southland team capable of beating any other province, which he achieved.

Booth also saw clearly the difference in attitudes between the New Zealand and English unions. After New Zealand had reinstated Karl Ifwersen at the end of the First World War, he argued that the English union lost a great opportunity by not reinstating its league players. Having the best players in rugby was 'a strong fighting factor' against the other game, he wrote.

There was not much in rugby that Booth — nicknamed 'the General' after the Salvation Army founder — did not do.

Booth was a popular man. 'He had no enemies,' the Dunedin *Evening Star* said when he died. 'His genial disposition won for him friends wherever he went.' Booth came of Yorkshire stock. His father David (1839–1916) was born near Halifax and said to have played for York. David was a cousin of Don Jowett, who played for Yorkshire and England.

DOCTOR'S CALL

Quite a few All Blacks over the years have played tests for both New Zealand and other countries; a smaller number have played tests both for and against their own country.

There could have been another to play against his own country, but he refused. Alfred Nolan Fell, known as Nolan, had played for Nelson (where his father was the mayor) and Otago then went to Edinburgh early in the twentieth century to further his medical studies. A versatile sportsman in both winter and summer, he made his debut for Scotland in 1901, the season when Scotland went through the Four Nations (as it was then) without a loss. The Scots beat Wales and Ireland then wrapped up the triple crown with an 18–3 win against England. That match was at Blackheath and is still Scotland's biggest win against the Auld Enemy on Sassenach soil.

Fell played an influential role. He figured in the play leading to two of the first-half tries and, playing on the right wing, crossed for Scotland's final score of the game. Fell thus became the first New Zealander to be in a winning triple crown team.

He also played for Scotland in the 1902 and 1903 championships but missed 1904 and 1905 because of injury. He was fit later in 1905, however, and was chosen to play against New Zealand. He withdrew a couple of days before the match, telling friends that he could not play against his homeland. Fell was never asked to play for Scotland again.

He had been the second New Zealander to play for Scotland. The first was John Anderson, who had been born in Edinburgh and his family moved to Christchurch when he was a toddler.

He returned to Scotland to be educated and played against England in 1872. Since he was less than a year old when he arrived in Christchurch, he qualified as a New Zealander and thus became the first to play a test match. He returned to Christchurch for a distinguished career in business and local body politics.

Fell remained in the United Kingdom for the rest of his life, working as a general practitioner in Colchester, Essex, where he was also one of the founders of the local rugby club and had two terms as its president. He served with the Royal Army Medical Corps during the First World War and a son, serving with the RAMC in the Second World War, died of wounds in North Africa in 1942.

BAD BLOOD?

Did a strange disciplinary hearing in 1911 that banned an All Black for twelve months have its origins in New Zealand's tour of the United Kingdom, Ireland and France in 1905–06? It may have.

Jimmy Duncan from Otago, who had captained New Zealand in its first test in 1903 and coached in the second, against Britain in 1904, was coach of the 1905–06 team. His appointment brought some protests, largely on the basis that the money spent on sending a coach would be better spent on sending another player. Reports about Duncan's acceptance and authority on the tour vary, but there was certainly some friction.

Five years later, Duncan refereed a club match involving his own club, Kaikorai, and one of its players was Alex McDonald, a member of the 1905–06 team. The night of the match, Duncan mentioned to the president of the Otago union, Frank Campbell, that McDonald during the match had said a word or words to him to which Duncan took exception. Campbell raised it at the next meeting of the Otago union management committee (of which Duncan was a member) and summonsed McDonald.

Local papers carried verbatim reports of the hearing which contained enough hints to suggest animosity between the two men. A subsequent letter to the editor confirmed it. One of several letters commented: 'A certain section of the committee appear to have taken upon themselves the functions of a tribunal of saints to inquire into the personal animosities existent or otherwise between Duncan and McDonald, and the generally level headed chairman showed a lapse from his usual discretion in allowing a childish tale received beforehand to outweigh his better judgment when the actual case was heard.'

McDonald appealed successfully against his suspension, the New Zealand union saying Duncan (who had taken no action on the field) had not followed correct procedure in just idly mentioning the incident to Campbell. The Otago union appealed against that, saying the NZRFU had exceeded its authority — far from the only time a provincial union made that particular accusation

— and asked what the English union would say. The NZRFU rather testily replied it had nothing to do with the RFU.

There the matter lay. McDonald continued to captain Kaikorai, Otago and New Zealand and he became a member of the Otago management committee. After the First World War, he moved to Wellington and became involved in administration and coaching, culminating in coaching the 1949 New Zealand team in South Africa.

A TIME TO ACT

When war came, rugby answered the call. Not because of any high-flown association between rugby and war, playing one in preparation for the other, as some people have written, but simply because in New Zealand a lot of young men who signed up also happened to be rugby players.

There would have been many reasons, such as a sense of adventure, mates signing up together, and some because they saw it as being the right thing to do.

A story that may be typical of rugby clubs in New Zealand is told in the museum at Riverton in Southland, a town rich in its own history and past importance, and now more a stopover on a tourist route. The museum there is one of the best regional museums in New Zealand, telling its story well without the cloying political correctness of some of its bigger colleagues.

The Riverton Football Club was given its own flag in 1913 by a member of a prominent family in the town, Annie McNaughton. Jim Cumming, one of the players then and a later life member, told the story of the flag in the club's centenary history (1974) and part of it is repeated on story boards in the museum. Wherever the players went, the flag was sure to go.

'When five of the players enlisted the day after war broke out in August 1914,' Cumming wrote, 'it mysteriously turned up in our tent at Tahuna Park in Dunedin.' (Tahuna Park was where recruits from Otago and Southland gathered before being shipped off.) 'Bill Morrin [another player] draped it outside the tent and any Rivertonian knew that it was a symbol of welcome and friendliness.'

The flag went off on the troopship to Egypt and Gallipoli. 'When I went back to Gallipoli a second time the flag was in the trenches at Courtney's Post. . . . When we were short of cleaning rags for rifles, strips were torn off for rifle cleaners — that was the last time I saw it in the war theatre but it went right through France and returned to Riverton, again in the hands of Bill Morrin.'

Another of the McNaughton family patched it up and the flag was tucked away in a drawer for many years before it was retrieved for display in the clubrooms. The club's history says: 'One hundred and twenty-eight men connected with the club joined the army and twenty-seven made the supreme sacrifice.' Riverton's population was about a thousand in 1909. The club's contribution, in terms of numbers and deaths, just about matches the national death ratio of about one in five.

IN TIME OF WAR

Many who played for their country also served it in times of war and many died for it. Among those who died while in uniform in the two world wars of the twentieth century were twenty All Blacks — thirteen in the First World War between 1914 and 1919 and seven in the Second, from 1939 until 1945. They were among 237 international rugby players to die in war.

The most prominent of the New Zealanders was Dave Gallaher, the captain of the first NZRFU team to play in the northern hemisphere, the landmark tour of 1905–06 in which the only loss was to Wales. Gallaher, who also served in the 1899–1902 Boer War, was later an Auckland and New Zealand selector. He enlisted for the First World War in 1916 and on 4 October 1917, during the attack on Gravenstafel Spur, a part of the Third Battle of Ypres, he was shot in the face and died a few hours later at an Australian casualty clearing station.

Not long before he was killed, Gallaher had written to a 1905 teammate, Ernie Booth. 'So far I have a whole skin,' he wrote, 'though life here on the whole is a matter of chance. So long "Old Horse", heaps of luck and good wishes from your old pal Dave.'

Booth wrote after hearing of Gallaher's death: 'Dave was a man of sterling worth, slow to promise, always sure to fulfil; guided by great determination and self-control, he was a valuable friend. In the huge list of fallen International Rugbyites in this gigantic fight of Right and Might, the name of Dave Gallaher among sportsmen-fighters stands out pre-eminently.'

Gallaher's name was perpetuated by the Gallaher Shield for club competition in Auckland and, more latterly, the Gallaher Cup for matches between New Zealand and France. Gallaher had captained the All Blacks against France in 1906, France's first full rugby international.

All Blacks teams in Europe have regularly made the trip to Nine Elms Cemetery in Belgium, where Gallaher is buried, beginning with the 1924 team when wreaths were laid by the captain, Cliff Porter, on behalf of New Zealand rugby, and by Fred Lucas, on behalf of Gallaher's Ponsonby club.

Dave Gallaher

One of Gallaher's 1905 teammates, Canterbury wing Eric Harper, also died in the First World War, shot dead during fighting near Jerusalem.

It's difficult to be definitive, but hundreds of provincial players also lost their lives in both world wars; as well as many players who had played club rugby.

SOMME CUP

Rugby matches in wartime, played by soldiers and with usually only soldiers as partisan spectators, engendered the same passions and enthusiasm as any matches at home between club or provincial rivals.

Army authorities saw the game as essential to the welfare of troops and there were periods in the First World War when soldiers would go almost straight from frontline duty to rugby, to either play or watch. The New Zealand Division team, sometimes called the Trench XV, played and beat a variety of opponents in 1917 but was not allowed to cross the Channel to meet the best British team, the Royal Army Service Corps, because of the exigencies of the service. (Preparation for the Messines battle came first.)

The alternative was an Easter Sunday match in Paris, sponsored by the newspaper *Le Journal*, with the idea of bringing some joy into Parisians' lives. The New Zealanders won 40–0 against a French team assembled specifically for the purpose, some of them leaving their military duties just the day before. The crowd was said by *Le Journal* to have been 60,000. The prize was a sculpture by a Parisian artist, Georges Chauvel, called 'Le Lanceur de Grenades', but it was soon dubbed the Somme Cup by the footballing soldiers.

One of the Division team, Reg Taylor, an All Black in 1913, was killed a few weeks later and another, Tom French, was wounded so badly he had to have an arm amputated. He was later a successful coach and a trophy named for him is awarded annually to the New Zealand Maori player of the year.

After the Armistice, the Division team and a team from troops stationed in Britain, the United Kingdom XV, came together in England and a New Zealand army team was chosen. It won the King's Cup tournament, sometimes described as rugby's first World Cup, from teams representing British services (called 'The Mother Country'), the Australian Imperial Force, the Canadian Expeditionary Force, the Royal Air Force, and South African Forces.

Other teams, representing battalions and other units, also played a wide range of matches in the United Kingdom while waiting for ships home.

The main New Zealand team toured South Africa on the way home, providing the first formal rugby contact between the two countries. They played fifteen matches for eleven wins, a draw and three losses. Although these matches were entirely army affairs and funded by governments, and had nothing to do with national rugby unions, they led directly to the first South African tour of New Zealand in 1921.

AID FOR SOLDIER

It's unusual for a club team to play a provincial team in New Zealand and unusual too for such a match to be preceded by a soccer game, but that's what happened at Carisbrook in Dunedin in September 1919.

There was a special reason. The two matches were staged to raise money for a soldier who had lost both eyes in the First World War. George Scott was an accomplished and popular fullback in club and provincial rugby before the war; he'd played twenty times for Otago and three times for the South Island.

When he first joined up, his rugby prowess was well known and while he still fulfilled military duties on the Western Front, he was chosen in the New Zealand Division team to play British and French sides in 1916. He was at fullback when the Divisional team, known as the Trench XV, beat a Welsh Division 18–3, but he was not available for the ultimate match of the short war season, against France in Paris for the Somme Cup.

A corporal in the Otago Battalion, he was shot in the head in the failed attack on Bellevue Spur (Passchendaele) on 12 October 1917, the day generally regarded as New Zealand's worst of the war, with more than 800 killed.

Scott was sent to hospitals in England as soon as his condition allowed and he, according to a letter home, 'took it very sore for a start to be blind'. But the outlook improved for him after treatment and rehabilitation at St Dunstan's, a specialist hospital for the blind. It got even better when he met one of the voluntary aides at the hospital, Lily Stubbings, who eventually returned to New Zealand as his wife.

Both rugby and soccer authorities decided Scott should be financially supported and a crowd of about 6000 showed up for the unusual double header. In the first game, an Otago soccer team beat a team of returned soldiers 6–3 (one of the goals was scored, incidentally, by Cecil Alloo, the only ethnic Chinese to be commissioned in the NZEF; Cecil and two brothers also played cricket for Otago, and one of them for New Zealand). In the second, a scratch Otago team beat Otago University, unbeaten for the year, 23–0.

The war never left Scott. He ran a poultry farm for a few years but had to give that up because of the effects of his wounds and he died in 1931, aged forty-two.

THE BOXING DUKE

When Hitler's deputy führer Rudolf Hess landed in Scotland on his bizarre mission at the height of German dominance during the Second World War, a former All Black, Brian McCleary, would have taken more than a passing interest.

Hess, whatever his aims, landed near the estate of Douglas Douglas-Hamilton, the Duke of Hamilton, the premier peer in Scotland, in 1941. Seventeen years before, when the duke was known as the Marquess of Douglas and Clydesdale, or just plain Dougie Hamilton, he wanted to get into the ring with McCleary, one of the 1924 All Blacks.

Hamilton was a well-known amateur boxer and he hung around with American Eddie Eagan, who was a Rhodes Scholar who won the light-heavyweight title at the 1920 Olympics. (He added a winter gold in bobsleigh in 1932.) McCleary had been both amateur and professional heavyweight champion of New Zealand in the early 1920s. He'd beaten one of his teammates, Maurice Brownlie, for the amateur title and as a pro, was cleaned out by Tom Heeney, another first-class rugby player, who fought Gene Tunney for the world title in New York in 1928. (Heeney had played for Poverty Bay.)

While the All Blacks were in Britain, the fighting lord proposed a bout with McCleary with funds raised to go to charity. McCleary declared himself willing, but rugby was the priority, a date couldn't be arranged and the idea lapsed. Two years later, Hamilton toured New Zealand 'for a look at the dominions' with Eagan and a couple of mates and again expressed interest in meeting McCleary in the ring. McCleary again said he was willing and that he was fit, but again the idea lapsed.

Hamilton went on his adventuring way, becoming one of two pilots in 1933 to fly over Mt Everest and thus the first to see at close range the summit of the world's highest mountain. He flew himself to Berlin three years later for the Olympics where he was at various political functions and may have met Hess (versions differ). He inherited the dukedom when his father died in 1940 and he served throughout the war in the RAF. He was also for a time president of the Hamilton Academy Former Pupils Rugby Club.

Brian McCleary

Three of the 1924 All Blacks, McCleary, Jack Steel and Jim Parker, were openly professional in other sports but they were as free as birds to play amateur rugby. South Africa during the 1920s asked the English union if a professional boxer could play rugby and it replied one could. The professional restriction applied only to league.

IN PRAISE OF GEORGE

Can any player — anyone in any sport — have been praised as eloquently as George Nepia was by the English novelist and artisan of words, Denzil Batchelor? Likely not.

Batchelor, as an eighteen-year-old undergraduate, saw Nepia play in 1924, which gave him an immediate advantage over people who have since written about him. Perhaps his best-known words about Nepia were these, written a quarter of a century later:

'If Mark Nicholls failed, there were others to improvise fresh attacks — if Nepia failed, the castle was taken, the side was beaten. . . . It is not with me a question of whether Nepia was the best fullback in history. It is a question as to which of the others is fit to loose the laces of his Cotton Oxford boots.'

Batchelor wrote that in 1949 in a book of reminiscing about sport he had seen, *Days without Sunset*.

He returned to Nepia in 1961 in his autobiography, *Babbled of Green Fields*. His praise of Nepia was more intense, but not so widely quoted. 'He seemed to be made of mahogany,' Batchelor wrote. 'His legs were new-stripped glistering tree-trunks . . . his short neck . . . would have buckled a guillotine.' He had the eyes of a falcon, the poise of a panther. 'He tackled with the sound of a thunderclap, and punted low and deep, gaining fifty yards with a wet, heavy ball with contemptuous ease in the teeth of a forward foot-rush. His unique

Charl Visser Collection

George Nepia attacks against the French Selection at Colombes Stadium in Paris in 1925.

52

feat was to gather a ball off the toes of a phalanx of forwards and — disdaining to fall on the ball — smash his way with it, generally backwards, through the whole ravening pack.'

New Zealand bothered to take only one fullback on the 1924 tour. 'If they had chosen one half as good as Nepia, he would have done the job for them,' Batchelor wrote.

Born of English parents in India and educated at Oxford, where he studied English literature, Batchelor began his writing career in Australia, working for the *Sunday Sun* in Sydney. When he returned to England in the late 1930s, he teamed up with multi-sportsman and writer, C.B. Fry, whose biography he wrote. After Batchelor died in 1969, an admirer wrote of him in *The Times* that 'he was one of those men who did so many different things well that he lacked the time (not the ability) to do one thing exceptionally well. He chose to diffuse his light rather than concentrate it.'

A HAKA'S WAKE

Of all the foreign appropriations of the haka, none could have been more bizarre than that by the eccentric Irish writer, James Joyce.

He lived in Paris for much of his adult life and according to various biographers, he was fond of rugby and keen on the Dublin club, Bective Rangers (on the evidence of the word 'Bective' appearing in each of his novels). He watched Ireland in Paris in 1923 and went to Colombes Stadium in 1925 for New Zealand's game against a French selection (the test was in Toulouse).

A few years later, when he was writing his novel *Finnegans Wake*, he remembered the haka. As luck would have it, he had a younger sister in Greymouth, Margaret Alice, who had joined the Convent of the Sisters of Mercy and was known as Sister Mary Gertrude. To Joyce and the rest of the scattered family, she was known as 'Poppie' (apparently because of a red cloak she wore when she was young and that gave her the appearance of a poppy).

Joyce wrote to her and asked if she could get the words to the haka for him.

It appears she copied them for him from the book of the tour by the All Black lock, Read Masters.

Having received the Maori, the half-blind Joyce then turned it into the strange form of English he adopted for *Finnegans Wake*. Various literary scholars since have spotted the remnants of the haka among Joyce's idiosyncratic language.

Finnegans Wake was at least seventeen years in the writing and was Joyce's last book, published in 1939, not long before his death in 1941. Although scholars have had difficulty working out precisely what it's about, its central theme seems to be a family, the Earwickers, the husband's non-specific transgression and how others in the family react to that. Here is a passage that appears to be based on the 1924 haka:

'Ko Niutirenis hauru leish! A lala! Ko Niutirenis haururu laleish! Ala lala! The Wullingund storm is breaking. The sound of maormaoring. The Wellingthund storm waxes fuercilier. The whackawhacks of the sturm. Kat ute ihis ihis! Katu te wana wana! The strength of the rawshorn generand is known throughout the world. Let us say if we may what a weeny wukeleen can do.

'Au! Au! Aue! Ha! Heish! A lala!'

This was apparently a reference to one of Joyce's characters, Buckley, shooting a Russian general during the Napoleonic wars.

There's also a theory that Joyce was taken with the All Blacks because they were called the Invincibles, a name that was associated with an Irish nationalist group in Dublin that was responsible for the murder in Phoenix Park, Dublin, of the Chief Secretary, Lord Cavendish, in 1882. In Joyce's mind and prose, the story goes, Phoenix Park became Colombes Stadium.

RADIO RUGBY

Rugby's popularity led to New Zealand being a pioneer in sports broadcasting. An enterprising Christchurch sports follower, 32-year-old Allan Allardyce, listened to crackly and hesitant broadcasts in the early days of radio and could see the potential. He persuaded the first company in the business, the Radio Broadcasting Company, that to broadcast a rugby match would increase interest in the new medium. He also persuaded the Canterbury Rugby Union that to allow a broadcast of one of its matches would increase interest in the game.

With a nod from both, he set up his rudimentary equipment in the back of the No. 1 stand at Lancaster Park on 29 May 1926 and commentated on a match between the Christchurch and High School Old Boys clubs. The experiment was deemed to be a success and there was even a report of one Lancaster Park neighbour putting a speaker on his garden wall so that passers-by could learn what was going on over the fence.

Years later, Allardyce said his debut broadcast was very well received — 'People said they were able to "see" the game through my commentary,' he remarked.

Not everyone was thrilled with the progress in communications. A few months later, the local referees' association complained to the Canterbury union: '. . . the association protests to the Canterbury Rugby Union against the radio broadcaster making continued personal comments on the rulings of referees'. Union committeemen seemed not to have been impressed. Jack Moloney asked with a laugh if the comment was fair and another said the broadcaster had as much right to criticise as did journalists at the game. The union took no action.

Allardyce continued with rugby but branched out to horseracing — broadcasting from a haystack outside the course — and public events, such as the arrival at Wigram of the Australian pilot, Charles Kingsford Smith, at the end of the first flight across the Tasman.

Allardyce's rugby commentaries were before the BBC made its entry into rugby broadcasting. Its first live sports broadcast came on 15 January 1927 when Teddy Wakelam called a Five Nations match from Twickenham between England and Wales. The first live soccer broadcast in England was a week later (between Arsenal and Sheffield Wednesday). (Wakelam, who had captained Harlequins, had more assistance than the lone wolf Allardyce. The *Radio Times* had published a diagram of Twickenham divided into numbered squares and during Wakelam's commentary, another voice would call out the number indicating which square play was in. This is one theory for the origin of the phrase, 'back to square one'.)

OLYMPIC RUGBY

New Zealand rugby players finally got to play at the Olympic Games when sevens was introduced at the Rio de Janeiro games in 2016.

Rugby, the full version, had been played at four previous Olympics — 1900, 1908, 1920 and 1924 — but no New Zealanders were involved. And unlike other major rugby playing countries, no All Black had ever competed at a games in some other sport.

Mark Irwin, a prop for New Zealand in twenty-five matches, including seven tests, got the closest. He was chosen in the New Zealand rowing eight for the games in Melbourne in 1956 but the eight didn't cross the Tasman because of a lack of funds.

Until 2016, the closest involvement any All Black had with the Olympics was by Jim Wylie, who toured North America with Australia in 1912 and New Zealand in 1913. He stayed on in California to study engineering at Stanford University where he teamed up with Australian Danny Carroll, who had been in the 1912 Australian rugby team (and the Australian team that won the Olympic gold in 1908 and the American team that won in 1920).

Wylie stayed in California when he graduated and coached Stanford in 1917 and then, from 1919 until he died in 1956, continued to select and coach teams at various levels. Wylie selected and coached, with Carroll and Harry Maloney of Stanford, the 1920 United States Olympic Games team, and with former Wallaby Pete Flanagan and Charlie Austin, the 1924 Olympic team. Wylie had been appointed co-coach with Austin of the team which went to the Paris Games, but he had to pull out for business reasons.

Among Wylie's last coaching tasks were for matches against Queen's University, Belfast (which included Jackie Kyle) in 1953 and the All Blacks in 1954.

Of Irish descent, Wylie played rugby for Auckland in 1910 and went to Sydney the following year and joined the Glebe club, which in 1912 won the Sydney grand final 6–5 over Western Suburbs. On the Wallaby tour to North America, Wylie broke ribs in the loss to Stanford and a bone in his hand in the ninth match, against University of California, the latter injury sidelining him for the last seven matches of the tour.

A fluent Maori speaker, Wylie acted as interpreter for Cook Islanders travelling to Tahiti with the Wallabies in 1912 and for Manawatu Maori performers at the 1915 Pan Pacific Exposition in San Francisco.

SEEING RED

It's often been written that Cyril Brownlie became the first player to be sent off in a rugby international when Welsh referee Albert Freethy told him to go early on in the test against England in 1925, the last of the Invincibles' matches in the United Kingdom — 'The Last of the Twenty-Eight', as the distinguished William Pember Reeves called it in a post-match poem.

Brownlie was one of four All Blacks to be sent off (Colin Meads 1967, Sonny Bill Williams 2017 and Scott Barrett 2019 were the others), but he was not the first in an international.

That dubious footnote belongs to an American, Ed Turkington, who was sent off for punching in a match against Romania at the Olympic Games in Paris in May 1924, about eight months earlier than the Brownlie dismissal.

It may be that the Americans, despite winning the gold medal, and the Romanians were not at the top of the rugby tree and that more highly rated rugby countries (including New Zealand) spurned the games, but the matches there were still official tests. The International Rugby Board, which at that stage of its existence was opposed to multi-team tournaments, gave the games an official nod by appointing referees, including Freethy. Rugby eighty years later could hardly hook up to the Olympic gravy train without coupling itself to the game's history in the Olympics.

The referee who dispatched Turkington was a Welshman, Charles Leyshon, who had settled in France, worked on the railways while he was a player there and was later an accountant. (Leyshon, a Freemason, was sent to Buchenwald concentration camp by the Germans during the Second World War and died there in 1944.)

Brownlie was unfortunate to even be the second — and for that matter to be the first sent off by Freethy. Freethy refereed the Olympic final between the United States and France and decided to send off French tight forward Marcel-Frédéric Lubin-Lebrère for swinging 'a hard Carpentier-like blow to Dick Hyland's jaw'. But the newspaper report, printed in several American papers, went on to say that Hyland's teammates implored Freethy to change his mind, which he did. One report quoted Freethy as saying: 'If you want him back, go and get him.'

Ron Palenski Collection

Referee Albert Freethy points and Cyril Brownlie begins his long Twickenham walk.

Perhaps Freethy learned a lesson in Paris because at Twickenham eight months later, he showed no intention of changing his mind.

The system of red and yellow cards was introduced to rugby in 2000 and the first All Black to be shown a yellow card was Anton Oliver, in a 2001 test against Argentina.

ONE-MATCH IFFY

For someone who played just once for the All Blacks, Karl Ifwersen cast a long shadow.

Paddy Sheehan, a player and journalist of long standing, once said of him: 'Karl was that class of footballer you get once in a decade.' Norm McKenzie, a coach and selector of various teams (including New Zealand) for about thirty years, called Ifwersen 'one of the most astute inside backs I have seen'.

Ifwersen played for Auckland as a teenager before the First World War; he switched to league and played for the national team, touring Australia in 1913. He had two separate stints away at the war and returned to league after it, playing seven tests for the Kiwis in all. He captained the Kiwis against Great Britain in 1920. (He was named a 'legend of league' by the New Zealand Rugby League in 2000.)

Early in 1921, Ifwersen decided to play rugby and the New Zealand Rugby Football Union reinstated him. The South Africans toured and with the series at one-all and one to play, the national selectors, George Nicholson, Donald Stuart and Alf Griffiths, dropped their captain, George Aitken (who later played for Scotland), and brought in Ifwersen.

His one game as an All Black was the scoreless draw on a rain- and windswept Athletic Park in Wellington.

'Iffy' was declared ineligible for the 1924–25 British tour because the NZRFU feared the English union might ban him because of his league background. But Ifwersen appeared in one of the trials in Auckland anyway, going on when Vic Badeley was injured, much to the delight of the crowd

Karl Ifwersen

and the chagrin of the union. Auckland crowds had a chant when Ifwersen was playing, 'Give it to Iffy.'

Ifwersen continued to play for another four years and later coached in Auckland and North Auckland. He wasn't always followed by just rugby headlines. He was the guilty co-respondent in a well-publicised divorce trial in 1919, he married three times, he was declared bankrupt ('He is a man who achieved fame too young,' the judge said) and he was convicted of theft as a servant.

Ifwersen was the grandson of a Danish sea captain who in the mid-nineteenth century plied the Tasman trade, especially transporting coal. In 1874, the British Government gave him a gold watch and the Shipwrecked Mariners' Society awarded him a silver medal after he saved more than forty passengers and crew from a British ship, the *Belle Isle*, that foundered in a gale the year before about 80 km east of Sydney.

COLOUR STORY

Until a few years ago, it had been assumed, logically enough, that the author of a tendentious article after the South Africans had played the national Maori team in 1921 was a South African.

After all, the reporter toured with the team as a representative of the *Johannesburg Star* and sent his dispatch to that paper. Unfortunately for him, the story was (illegally) leaked from the telegraph office and published in New Zealand.

The reporter, identified at the time only as C. Blackett, wrote it was 'the most unfortunate match ever played . . . bad enough having play team officially designated New Zealand natives, but spectacle thousands Europeans frantically cheering on band of coloured men to defeat members of own race was too much for Springboks, who frankly disgusted'.

There was more in the same vein in the story that was first published in the Napier *Daily Telegraph* then circulated throughout New Zealand. Outrage piled upon outrage and the South African manager, Harold Bennett, tried to distance himself and the team from the report. He even said Blackett was sorry, but Blackett retorted he was not sorry at all.

'What I do regret,' he said, '. . . is the mutilated and abridged form in which it was published in certain papers for reasons best known to themselves. . . . Persons who surreptitiously obtained and disseminated the cable only published those passages which could be construed as an attack on the Maoris.'

(Some telegraph workers were sacked for leaking the cable, but they were later reinstated.)

It was not the only racial issue on that tour but was the most publicised (and probably the most remembered).

Blackett was not a South African. He was Australian. He'd been born in Tasmania in 1881, worked for a time in New Zealand where he had relatives and stayed in South Africa after serving in the Boer War. He also served for a time in 1915 in South-West Africa before returning to Australia and joining the Australian Imperial Force, with which he remained for the rest of the war, ending up on General John Monash's staff and being made a Member of the Order of the British Empire.

He returned to his Johannesburg post after the war and aside from tours such as that in New Zealand in 1921, remained there until his death from pancreatic cancer in 1938. (Blackett also dipped a toenail in first-class cricket, being called from the press box to fill in for South Africa against Western Province.) His death was widely reported in New Zealand but made no mention of his story from Napier seventeen years before.

A SPECIAL HAKA

The name of Wiremu Rangi is linked forever with the Invincible All Blacks of 1924–25.

Rangi, a farmer from the east coast of the North Island, was one of several supporters who paid for the privilege of travelling with the team and being included in all team arrangements. Another was Frank Acheson, a Native Land Court judge who took immense pride in the fact one of the players, Les Cupples, was a nephew.

To while away the long sea hours as the ship bore them across the Pacific, Acheson at the invitation of the ship's master gave lectures to passengers about Maori lore. One of his lectures was about haka and the different roles they play in Maori life. The players decided they wanted one specific to them as well as the 'Ka Mate' haka which had come to be associated with the All Blacks.

Acheson was travelling second class on the ship and Rangi third, but somehow they overcame the rigidities of the upstairs-downstairs mentality and got together to write a haka. The first draft was Rangi's, then Acheson added

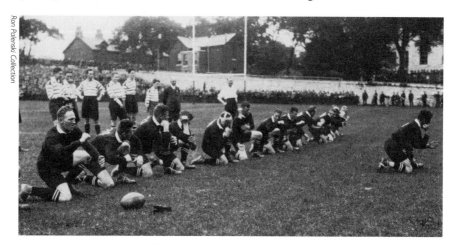

Ron Palenski Collection

George Nepia leads the All Blacks in their new haka in the opening match of the 1924 tour, against Devon.

words here and there and when they'd agreed on the words, Rangi was left to devise the actions. The All Blacks performed it first in public when they arrived in Plymouth.

Rangi, like about a dozen of the All Blacks, had served in the First World War; a gunshot wound to a leg on Gallipoli in 1915 meant he was invalided home, but when he'd recovered he signed up again and spent the rest of the war in Europe.

Some time after the 1924–25 tour, he took up residence in Sydney, where he was evidently well known as Bill Rangi, a welcoming New Zealand face to visitors passing through. He popped up at rugby and rowing matches and was on the wharf when the New Zealand Maori team left for France in 1926. The Maori did a haka from the stern of the ship and Rangi led a waiata in response.

Rangi was also there in the forefront when the aviation pioneer, Francis Chichester, landed in Sydney after a 36-hour flight from Croydon in South London in 1930. Rangi was one of those who greeted Chichester with a haka and then he and a couple of others hoisted Chichester up on their shoulders. (Chichester gained a later fame in 1966–67 when he sailed single-handed around the world; he'd immigrated to New Zealand in 1919 and stayed about ten years).

Rangi must have been troubled by the legacy of his war wounds because he was a member of the New South Wales Totally and Permanently Disabled Soldiers' Association. He died in 1952.

MORMON INFLUENCE

Rugby has often been called a religion in New Zealand, such has been the enduring devotion of people to the game, creating their own playing gods to worship. But the real religions have had a profound influence — the Marist Brothers and other Roman Catholic orders, and the Church of England and Presbyterians through schools.

The Church of Jesus Christ of Latter-day Saints, the Mormons, have also had significant influence. It's well known that some players, Sid Going and Steve Pokere in particular, were Mormons, whose rugby lives were influenced by their devotion.

Perhaps less known is the profound Mormon influence on a man still regarded as one of the greatest of All Blacks, George Nepia. He gave much credit to a Mormon missionary at Maori Agricultural College at Bridge Pa, Hastings by the name of Erwin Ulrich Moser (1899–1995), who was more often known simply as Elder Moser.

He and other missionaries from Utah spent almost three years in New Zealand in the early 1920s. Gordon Young, a grandson of the Mormon church leader Brigham Young, once said Nepia told him: 'All I know about rugby I learned from Elder Moser.'

Coming from an American football background, Moser among other things taught Nepia how to put spin on the ball when he kicked it, increasing accuracy and range.

Nepia wrote in a newspaper article in the 1930s that when he saw Moser impart spin on the ball when throwing it, he knew it could be adapted to rugby. 'A spinning ball would, I reckoned, be difficult to field and could, with sufficient control, be made to bounce in direction at will.'

Nepia said it took him two years to perfect the kick. 'I spent every spare minute trying to get it, but it eluded me so long that even my best school friends began to call me crazy for worrying about it.' But eventually it came, and it served him well 'thousands of times' on the playing fields of New Zealand, Australia and Britain.

After his time in New Zealand, Moser lived the rest of his life in Cache Valley, an agricultural area that straddles northern Utah and south-east Idaho.

The Maori Agricultural College, opened in 1912, closed in 1931 after its buildings were severely damaged in the Hawke's Bay earthquake. The centre of Mormon influence on rugby later moved to Church College in Hamilton, which has had four future All Blacks pass through its ranks, Sid and Ken Going, Norm Berryman and Jamie Joseph.

ARTHUR'S HISTORY

When teenager Arthur Swan went off to war in 1918, his occupation was listed as salesman. The war, though, was the first the public was to see of what became his vocation, finding out facts and compiling lists.

While serving mostly in England, he started, entirely unofficially, a history of the New Zealand Expeditionary Force; it lies fallow in the Alexander Turnbull Library in Wellington. He played rugby for a time in Gisborne, became a referee and was handicapper for the local athletics and cycling club. He compiled his own list of Olympic Games results (and that lies in the New Zealand Rugby Museum), but it was rugby's facts and figures that were his enduring love.

He moved around the country and settled in Wellington where he teamed up with another enthusiast, Arthur Carman, and together they produced the first *Rugby Almanack* (with All Blacks lock Read Masters adding profile weight to the cover). The two Arthurs also worked together in Carman's bookshop in Wellington, which was something of a gathering place for rugby gossip and fact-finding. When Carman was in jail during the Second World War for breaching emergency regulations (he was a pacifist), Swan kept the shop going and delivered *Almanack* proofs to his incarcerated editor.

Swan's magnum opus was the two-volume *History of New Zealand Rugby Football* (commissioned by the NZRFU), but there was much else besides. There were also provincial and club histories and

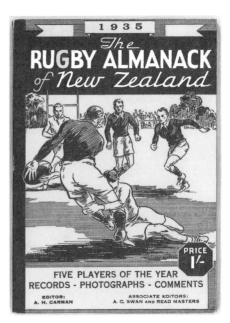

The first fruit of Arthur Carman and Arthur Swan's labours.

many newspaper articles, in one of which he described the 1888 Natives as the best team to tour in New Zealand's name. With no digital finding aids, he pored over newspapers in the Parliamentary Library in Wellington (where the librarian, Guy Scholefield, was an empathetic observer), and several times he toured New Zealand, seeking out bound newspaper volumes in public libraries and in newspaper offices.

Swan was made official historian by the NZRFU and given life membership in 1968. He died five years later, on 15 November 1973. He was never known publicly as anything but Arthur Swan — or, in the age of initials in sports writing, A.C. Swan — but his name at birth was Arthur Bluett. His father Richard Henry Bluett died when he was three, and mum Alice remarried two years later, to Hector Percy Swan, so Arthur, by then nearly six, became Arthur Swan. The name was never changed legally, but Arthur stated his preference was to be a Swan, and this is noted on his army service record.

TRY ON CANVAS

Sport and art in modern times are often seen as being on opposite sides of the cultural fence, giving rise to a belief that people follow one or the other, but not both. Yet the two have been linked for centuries, sport providing inspiration for artists and sculptors in the ancient worlds but not so much the modern.

Before photographs began to be widely used in newspapers in the early twentieth century, artists were often employed, especially in Britain, to portray scenes from great sporting occasions. Some rugby illustrations were brought together in an exhibition in London in early 1925, perhaps to take advantage of the presence of the All Blacks.

A noted art critic of the time, Frank Rutter, wrote that the exhibition 'incidentally exposed the lamentable blindness of our painters and sculptors to the pictorial and plastic possibilities of this great game'. Amid them all, he wrote, there was only one real picture and that was a 'spirited water colour' by Frank Gillett of the All Blacks' match against Wales in 1905, showing Teddy

Morgan of Wales scoring the only try of the match.

The painting was titled 'The Try That Beat New Zealand' and Rutter said the 'action and dash of Morgan is rendered with a convincing fidelity that must satisfy the most exacting rugger enthusiast'. An All Black is seen lunging too late at Morgan and that is likely to be the artist's All Black namesake, fullback George Gillett.

At the time of the match, Frank Gillett worked for the weekly *Graphic* magazine in London and later branched out to contribute to a wide range of publications on any number of subjects, including illustrating adventure stories for boys.

Gillett also painted a scene from the All Blacks' match against England, showing Billy Stead receiving the ball from Teddy Roberts in a move that led to one of Duncan McGregor's four tries. There was also a scene from the first test of the 1905 tour, against Scotland, showing Ernest Simson kicking a dropped goal for the home team.

Gillett lived in the small Suffolk town of Beccles later in life and died in hospital in 1927, two years after the London exhibition. The Welsh match painting is now in the National Museum of Wales. Two of Gillett's rugby works, incidentally, were entered in the arts competition at the Olympic Games in Amsterdam in 1928, which made him one of that rarest of species, a posthumous Olympian.

HOLY ORDERS

There was much that was unusual about rugby in the 1920s when the game re-established itself after the First World War and coped with the fact rugby in Australia was virtually confined to New South Wales.

As a way of helping our mates across the Tasman, the NZRFU agreed to 'test' matches every year against the New South Wales state team (Queensland having gone into abeyance for a decade).

These matches led to some unusual All Blacks selections, among them the

Paul Kane

choice of the only two Roman Catholic priests to play for New Zealand. The first of them was Paul Kane, a centre or second five-eighth who had played for West Coast and moved to Wellington in 1921. Playing under his mother's maiden name of Markham, he captained Wellington at times and was the New Zealand centre against New South Wales in 1921. He also played for Wellington against South Africa that year. The church came first and he was soon lost to the game, following his vocation as a parish priest.

Two years later, Father Patrick McCarthy, a halfback for the Marist club in Christchurch, played just two games for Canterbury, was then picked by the South Island selectors and, on such a lean first-class diet, found himself playing for New Zealand against New South Wales.

As with Kane, he had to soon put the game behind him, and he later served as a parish priest in Australia.

A reserve in each of the test matches against South Africa in 1937, Frank Green, was ordained as a Presbyterian minister in 1940.

One of the All Blacks in South Africa in 1949, Ian Botting, went on to Oxford University to study theology and was later ordained as a Church of England minister. He played for England against Wales and Ireland in 1950 and the International Rugby Board, as it then was, decreed that never again would someone be able to play for any of the 'home' countries after first playing for one of 'the dominions'.

Several ordained men have played first-class rugby including for New Zealand Maori. The Rev. Ngatai Wanoa was a regular in the great Hawke's

Bay pack of the 1930s and played for the national Maori team against Great Britain in 1930. He suffered the indignity for a cleric of being ordered off in a Ranfurly Shield match against Southland. Another celebrated Maori rugby player and later minister was Muru Walters, who became a bishop.

THE BOXER

Arthur Harding was a forward who toured New Zealand in 1904 with a Great Britain team, played for Wales against New Zealand in 1905 and captained the Anglo-Welsh team that toured in 1908. Throughout his career, he was known as 'Boxer'.

There's a hint that he may have lived up to the nickname during the 1908 tour. According to a little-known newspaper published in Dunedin at the time, Harding and the New Zealand captain, Freddy Roberts, came to blows during a jaunt to Waihola, a lakeside hamlet just south of Dunedin.

The Anglo-Welsh played Otago then went to Invercargill to play Southland but Harding, needing medical treatment, stayed in Dunedin, where the first test was to be played a week later. Filling in time, Harding joined some of the New Zealand players on their day trip to Waihola and the incident supposedly occurred, for no known reason. The story appeared in a column by 'Murphy' (otherwise unidentified) in the *Weekly Budget*, a short-lived weekly newspaper, of which just a few copies survive.

The contretemps, if such it was, couldn't have done much harm to Harding's standing because he returned to New Zealand the following year, getting a job in Wellington as an administrative assistant to Tom Wilford (later Sir Thomas), a lawyer-politician with a great love of rugby. Harding became secretary of the Welsh Society in Wellington and he continued to play rugby. His patron, Wilford, had a sister, Izie; they were engaged early in 1915 and married five months later. (It seems likely that Harding met Wilford and his 28-year-old sister during the tour. Another British player, Henry Vassall, met his future wife on that tour and yet another, Percy Down, forgot to let go of a woman's hand when the ship was leaving and fell into the water, to be rescued by, among others, All Blacks George Gillett and Arthur Francis.)

Harding became a farm manager in the Wanganui area and all the while continued to play club and social (The Law versus Insurance, for example) rugby. He was picked to play for Wanganui in 1913 but a broken shoulder blade in a fall from a horse delayed his Wanganui debut for a year. Harding later moved to another farm job in Wairarapa. He died in 1947, aged sixty-eight.

A son, Frederick, won a Military Cross in the Second World War when serving with the New Zealand Artillery in North Africa.

'Boxer' Harding is not to be confused with Rowe Harding, who played for Wales (including against New Zealand in 1924) and the British Isles. He was a great-uncle of the 2002 All Black, Sam Harding.

ROYAL RIDE

The national Maori team gained an unexpected fellow passenger when they travelled to Wales by train on their worldwide tour in 1926–27.

Manager Ned Parata had received a telegram from the mayor of Newport, saying that the Duke of York — the future King George VI and the Queen's father — would be meeting the players at the Newport station.

But more than just meeting, the royal carriage was hooked up to the team's train as it carried on into Wales. Parata and captain Wattie Barclay were invited into the royal carriage to meet the Duke and the three of them had a smoke and a chat while the players lined up in the passageway outside, holding out notebooks and bits of paper for the royal signature. He signed them all with a shaky 'Albert' because, as Barclay recalled, 'the train was travelling flat out and rolling quite a bit'.

'Bertie', as he was known, knew his rugby. He may have told Parata and Barclay that he saw the New Zealand Army team at Twickenham in 1919 when it won the King's Cup; the Duke of York was there with his father, King

George V, and his older brother, the Prince of Wales.

It may be little known but the future king's knowledge of rugby went beyond watching the odd game. One of his closest confidants was Louis Greig, a doctor who had played for Scotland against New Zealand in 1905. He was said to have been a more influential advisor to the Duke than Lionel Logue, the speech therapist who helped him overcome a stammer and whose story was told in the 2010 film *The King's Speech*.

Greig and the Duke met at the Royal Naval College in 1909 when Albert was thirteen and Greig twenty-seven and the college surgeon. Despite the difference in age and status, the pair seemed to get on famously; where one went, the other seemed to also go. They served on ships together, they were in the air force together — 'Bertie' was the first royal to earn his wings — and played at Wimbledon in the men's doubles. They were beaten in the first round by the veteran pair of Arthur Gore and Roper Barrett, both former champions. 'Bertie' is the only member of the royal family to have competed in a grand slam tennis tournament. King George V called Greig his diffident and shy son's 'tonic'. Greig was influential in Bertie's choice of wife, Elizabeth Bowes-Lyon, and dandled the first child, Princess Elizabeth (the future Queen), on his knee.

VERSATILE MAORI

A couple of the Maori players who played in France and the United Kingdom in 1926–27 had more than just rugby to their credit.

One of them, Jack Macdonald, also rowed at the Olympic and Empire Games (as well as having a distinguished league career). Another, Dick Pelham, won a national swimming title the year before the tour and, during it, won an invitation swimming race at Clermont-Ferrand. When he'd finished with rugby and competitive swimming, he turned to surf lifesaving and won the national individual surf race in 1937 and was in a New Zealand team that went to Australia in 1938.

Born in Rotorua in 1901, Pelham was a bit of a wanderer in his teenage years and did not play his first organised game of rugby until 1921. Swimming took him to Auckland, but he continued rugby, playing for Ponsonby and Auckland. After the French tour, he stayed in Wellington, playing for the Athletic club and Wellington as well as New Zealand Maori, including the 13–19 loss to Great Britain in 1930.

Pelham was a taxi driver in Wellington until he and his wife Margery returned to Rotorua in 1971. It was Dick Pelham who drove broadcaster Peter Sellers to Athletic Park the day of the second test in 1956. They went to the Adelaide Road side of the ground (the Western Bank side) and Pelham waited while Sellers interviewed people queuing to get into the ground. When Sellers decided to saunter across the ground to see the ladies preparing the pies, Pelham went off looking for other fares. Sellers interviewed Dulcie Kilby, the wife of former All Blacks captain Frank, and asked how many pies would be sold that day. She replied with a specific and large number, to which Sellers made his infamous retort: 'That's a bloody lot of pies.' His swearing on air was uncommon for the time, but he escaped censure.

Macdonald was one of the solid branches of the Macdonald whanau of Marlborough, a family that has contributed much talent to the rugby world. Of more recent times, Leon Macdonald and Hoani Macdonald are descendants, as is Jamie Joseph, whose mother was a Macdonald.

Jack Macdonald won gold and silver medals in the rowing four and eight at the first Empire Games, in Hamilton, Ontario in 1930, and was also in the New Zealand eight at the Olympic Games in Los Angeles in 1932; he carried the flag in the opening ceremony.

One of many considered unlucky not to be an All Black, he switched to league with the London club Streatham and Mitcham in the mid-1930s then went back to rugby when he served with the RAF in the Second World War. He played in one wartime international, thus becoming the first Maori to play for England; and played for the RAF and the Dominions. He also played tennis for New Zealand Services. Brothers Enoka and Manny were also accomplished players in both forms of rugby.

BATTLE ON TWO FRONTS

The Battle of Solway is a phrase laden with emotion from rugby's past. It refers to a Ranfurly Shield match at Solway Showgrounds in Masterton on 9 July 1927 when Hawke's Bay took the shield from Wairarapa 21–10.

Several weeks later, Wairarapa regained the shield in the committee room when the NZRFU and its appeal council ruled that Hawke's Bay had fielded an ineligible player, Wattie Barclay. (Barclay was a Bay player but had been in Auckland where he played for College Rifles and was a reserve for Auckland before he returned home; the issue was whether he was home in time to be eligible. The Bay thought he was; the NZRFU thought otherwise.)

That was the verbal battle.

The physical battle was during the game, although accounts vary, as they usually do, about how much of a battle it really was; whether it was a typically hard game or a dirty game. Two New Zealand teammates from the 1924 northern hemisphere tour, Maurice Brownlie and Quentin Donald, were sent

With what seems plenty of support, Maurice Brownlie dribbles downfield against Wairarapa.

off after what the local paper described as a 'rough-up'. Brownlie and Donald sat together on the touchline and watched the rest of the game, chatting away, seemingly happily.

A spectator who knew what he was talking about, George Uttley, was headmaster at Wairarapa College (and had played for Otago and North Otago). He said if what he saw was to be the norm for rugby, he would consider introducing soccer to his school and may advise boys not to play rugby after school.

Yet players did not think the game was anything out of the ordinary (which of course it may not have been). Barclay, the man at the centre of the eligibility fuss, told journalist-author Lindsay Knight in 1980 that it had been 'a good, hard game. I don't think there was any ill feeling among the players.'

Another noteworthy feature of the match was the McKenzie brothers. Bert McKenzie was the referee, brother Norm selected and coached Hawke's Bay and another brother, Ted, selected and coached Wairarapa. Ref McKenzie resigned as secretary of the Wairarapa referees' body because the Wairarapa union had dismissed the charge against Donald as being frivolous; the union didn't back its man. Back in the Bay, Brownlie also got off.

There was a story, often repeated but with no evidence, that the chairman of the NZRFU, Stan Dean, was at the match and advised Wairarapa to protest about Barclay's presence on the field. When the case went to the union, Dean presided and Norm McKenzie argued one way and brother Ted the other. It eventually went to the union's appeals council.

In the meantime, Wairarapa had lost to Manawhenua (a short-lived combination of Manawatu and Horowhenua) so the shield had to be quietly delivered to Palmerston North.

STREET RIOTS

It's a well-known story that Ian Kirkpatrick and Bryan Williams were caught up in a street riot in Cape Town during the All Blacks' tour in 1976 and felt a blast of police teargas. Journalist Bob Howitt and photographer Ross Wiggins were with them at a city centre book signing. Police got them out of it, let them recover in a police vehicle, then returned them to the team's hotel.

What's perhaps less well known is that some earlier All Blacks, especially Geoff Alley, Jim Burrows and Neil McGregor, were also caught up in a riot, also in Cape Town, during the 1928 tour.

They were known as the 'flag riots' because they marked the day on which the 'old' South African flag was first used or, as Burrows wrote, 'when the Dutch Union flag was officially hoisted alongside the Union Jack'. (This was the official Union of South Africa flag that lasted until 1961, when it became the republic's flag and was in use until the end of 1994.)

Jim Burrows

Burrows said people were running around pulling the flags down and clashing with police.

'Geoff Alley has in his room now half a brick which smashed through the window at the back of the car he was riding in. In another car, Neil McGregor was struck on the shoulder, but fortunately he was not injured. Mac is keeping that stone as a memento of Cape Town.'

Burrows said that about eight of the All Blacks went into town at night to have a look at the riots and became alarmed when they heard a cry, 'Come on the All Blacks.' They wondered if any of their teammates had become involved, but it soon became clear that a group of the rioters had given themselves the name 'All Blacks'. Burrows also noted that the name 'All Blacks' misled some people at first. 'A remark was overheard at the hotel the other night — an old lady was speaking, "But they speak perfect English, don't they?"'

Burrows was later a distinguished soldier during the Second World War, was rector of Waitaki Boys' High School and commanded the army Kayforce during the Korean War in the early 1950s.

Alley was one of a family of high achievers. A brother was Rewi Alley, a noted Sinophile who spent most of his life in China; two sisters, Gwen and Joy, were respected educationalists, Gwen in the field of early childhood and Joy as a nurse educator. Geoff Alley himself became New Zealand's first national librarian.

BOOTS 'N' ALL

Boots were the tyres on which football developed. The more serious about the game players became, the fussier they were about their boots.

One home-grown brand dominated the market for perhaps sixty or seventy years of the twentieth century. The brand was O'B and the company was founded by Michael O'Brien, who had left County Clare in about 1860 to seek his fortune in the Victorian goldfields and continued his search across the Tasman on the West Coast. He set up a bootmaking shop in Greymouth and after a few years crossed the Alps to found M. O'Brien and Co. in Christchurch.

The business grew and grew. One of Michael's sons, Arthur, was packed off to London to train as a doctor and he came home in 1904 as captain-manager of the British rugby team, the All Blacks' first test opponents. (By marketing alchemy, the team is now regarded as one of the British and Irish Lions sides and O'Brien could claim to be Lion No. 115.) When Michael died, Arthur eventually inherited the business which flourished until the 1960s, when it appears to have suffered from imported opposition. (Arthur had died in 1951.)

The company was among the first to use All Blacks to promote its goods. 'George Nepia wore OB Football Boots throughout the Australian and English tours,' one advertisement crowed. 'He says they stood up to the severest tests . . .' They did not seem to impress the NZRFU chairman, Stan Dean, though, because he favoured a pair he'd seen in England when managing the All Blacks.

He ordered some for the All Blacks' tour of South Africa in 1928, which prompted criticism from journalists and other manufacturers.

'Those worn by both 1905 and 1924 All Blacks were good enough for victory. Why not now?' asked *NZ Truth*. The Manufacturers' Association said it viewed with alarm that the team would tour with foreign boots. An aggrieved writer of a letter to the editor of the *Otago Daily Times* wondered if Dean knew that some great players (Bob Whiteside, 'Barlow' Madigan, Billy Stead) had been bootmakers. In any case, it was not who made the boots that mattered, but the men inside them.

A few months later though, Dean appears to have backed off because M. O'Brien and Co. ran an advertisement which said: 'Every member of the 1928 All Blacks team will play in the OB Football Boots during their tour.'

UNCLE SAM ALL BLACKS

Americans have played for the All Blacks. That's from the strange but true file.

Two of them, seventy or so years apart. Most people would see this odd couple as Samoan but, technically, they were Americans because they were born in Pago Pago, the capital of American Samoa, about 85 km south-east of Samoa.

The first of the American All Blacks, Frank Solomon, could have been nicknamed 'Milestone': he was the first Samoan to play for New Zealand, he was the last wing forward to play for New Zealand and he was the first Samoan to play for New Zealand Maori (because that's what the selectors thought he was).

Solomon, whose half-brother David was also an All Black, was at wing forward in the test against Australia in Auckland in 1931 and the following year, after the NZRFU had abolished the wing forward position, he played two tests at number eight in the first Bledisloe Cup series in Australia.

Solomon was a well-known man about rugby in Auckland (aside from a stint in Gisborne when he coached Poverty Bay) and a stalwart of Ponsonby. Another Ponsonby fixture, Sir Bryan Williams, remembered the Solomons from

Dave Solomon

Frank Solomon

his younger days, something others clearly didn't because Williams was frequently described as the first with Pacific Island blood to play for New Zealand. But that honour belonged to Tongan-born Walter Batty, an Auckland contemporary of the Solomons who first played for the All Blacks in 1928. Batty also played against the British Isles in 1930. Like Maori players such as George Nepia and Jimmy Mill, he was excluded from selection for the New Zealand tour of South Africa in 1928 because of his ethnicity.

Another of islands origin who preceded Williams was Arthur Jennings from Bay of Plenty. Born in Fiji, he played six matches for the All Blacks in 1967.

The other American was of the modern generation: Jerome Kaino, who played in eighty-three tests including the World Cup wins of 2011 and 2015.

Kaino's family was from Samoa but finding few opportunities, moved across the water to American Samoa and he was born in the Lyndon B. Johnson Medical Center in Pago Pago. 'That's why I'm technically American,' he once wrote. 'I even have an American passport.'

The family moved to New Zealand in 1987 when Kaino was four years old. Kaino noted that was the year the All Blacks won the first World Cup — 'I don't remember anything about travelling over. I was too small.'

ORIENTAL MASTER

When Arthur Percy Singe died in January 1936, aged just thirty-seven, obituaries in the two Auckland papers noted he had been a prominent footballer who made his name in the army teams during the First World War.

He'd been in the New Zealand Division team that won the King's Cup in

1919 and then toured South Africa. All of that was true. But there was much that was not written.

For a start, his birth surname was Sing, not Singe. He was half-Chinese. And he had been banned from two sports — rugby and league.

William Ping Sing was born in China and immigrated to New Zealand, where he married Frances Margaret Smith, who was of Irish heritage. They had four sons, all of whom served in the war.

Arthur joined in 1915 as a driver and later transferred to the post and telegraph section, serving continuously until football took him to South Africa and home. His service record shows his surname as both Sing and Singe, and sometimes the latter with an official's stroke through the 'e'. The South African Rugby Board put a stop to two non-whites, Arthur Wilson (whose father was a Barbadian) and Parekura Tureia (a Maori) being on the tour, but it made no mention of Sing(e). (Ironically, Tureia captained the national Maori team against South Africa in 1921, the match that so annoyed an Australian-born Johannesburg journalist, Mort Blackett.)

Singe, as he was now regularly known, played for the Marist club and for Auckland in 1920 but the following year was spotted playing league. The New Zealand union in Wellington was told and it instructed the Auckland union to 'fulfil its obligations', which it apparently did. He was soon playing regularly for a league club, Marist Old Boys, and for Auckland.

He was a member of the New Zealand league team on its infamous tour of Britain in 1926–27, the 'tour that died of shame', to use the title of John Coffey's book about it. It was an unhappy tour, largely because of the domineering antics of its Australian coach, Ernest Mair. Seven of the players refused to play while Mair continued to be involved — among them were Singe and a former All Black, Phonse Carroll. The seven were subsequently banned for life (the ban was rescinded by the New Zealand Rugby League in 1962).

Sing was one of the few men of Chinese descent to play rugby at a high level in New Zealand. Another was Arthur Fong of Greymouth and he also became a test referee.

JERSEY TRAGEDY

Horsing around over a souvenired Australian jersey the night of the Wallabies' 31–6 win against New Zealand Maori in Palmerston North in 1936 cost one of the Maori players his life.

Bernie Rogers, twenty-four, who'd played on the side of the scrum, and close friend Hawea Mataira were in the team's hotel, had had a few drinks, and each claimed ownership of an Australian jersey gained in a swap that afternoon.

Rogers fell and banged his head on a concrete floor. He was taken to hospital where the next morning the initial report was that although he was still unconscious, it was expected he would recover. But he died early in the afternoon.

In Gisborne, where Rogers lived, the *Poverty Bay Herald* reported: 'Deep consternation has been caused among the Maoris of Poverty Bay by the incident, more especially as telephonic inquiries made late this morning established the fact that the injured player was considered to have only the slightest chance of recovery. His young wife [Hinepaku], a daughter of Mr Turoa Pohatu, Manutuke, left Gisborne for Rotorua this morning to join her husband's family. Mr and Mrs Rogers have been married only a year, the wedding having taken place shortly after the return of the Maori All Blacks team from its Australian tour at the close of the 1935 rugby season.'

The Maori team manager, Kingi Tahiwi, said Rogers and Mataira were the best of friends and were merely skylarking.

'Ned' Parata, the 'father' of Maori rugby and chairman of selectors, told the inquest two days later that he had last seen Rogers about eight o'clock on the night of the match. 'I left the hotel and about an hour later I was notified of an accident. . . . I immediately returned but by this time the injured man had been taken to the hospital.'

Rogers played for Poverty Bay, had previously played for Bay of Plenty and had played in All Blacks trials. Mataira had been an All Black two years before, going on the 1934 tour of Australia. He later played league and went on the

1939 English tour that was abandoned because of the Second World War.

One of Mataira's younger brothers, Tony, was also a notable rugby player and appeared for New South Wales Country against the British Isles in Canberra in 1950. Mataira, who was a twenty-year-old cadet at the Royal Military College, Duntroon, scored Country's only points, a penalty goal, in a 47–3 loss. Mataira, later a lieutenant-colonel, served in Malaya, Singapore and Vietnam.

OBO'S PAIR

Alexander Obolensky played just four times for England. Yet there's a restaurant named after him at Twickenham, there's a statue of him at Ipswich in Suffolk, he wasn't English and his most celebrated moment is on YouTube.

His fame rests squarely on the two tries he scored against New Zealand on 4 January 1936, giving England their first win against the All Blacks and their only one until 1973.

The match remains known as 'Obolensky's match'. He scored midway through the first half and then again just before halftime. It wasn't so much that he scored, but how he scored.

The *Morning Post* provided an admiringly graphic description: 'Runners we have seen before but never such a runner with such an innate idea of where to go and how to get there. His double swerve to gain his first try was remarkable enough but the extraordinary turn-in and diagonal right to left run which won him his second which drew forth that great Twickenham rarity, a double roar of applause, will never be forgotten by anybody who saw it.' (A double roar comprised the roar when the try was scored and the second when the scorer, head modestly bowed, retreated into his own half to await the restart.)

Obolensky was a Russian prince whose family fled their homeland in 1919 in the wake of the revolution. He had not been naturalised a British citizen at the time of the All Blacks match and this apparently led to an

Prince Alexander Obolensky

exchange with the Prince of Wales (later King Edward VIII) before the game. The prince (apparently) asked Obolensky what qualified him to play for England. 'Obo', one prince to another, replied: 'I am a student at Oxford University, sir.'

Though his fame was enduring, his career was not. He did not score again in three more matches for England though while on tour in South America with a British invitation team he was reported to have scored seventeen tries in one match against Brazil. Reports of that are contradictory, however.

Obolensky did not live long to enjoy his fame. He was practising take-offs and landings in a Hurricane fighter on an aerodrome in Suffolk on 29 March 1940, when one of the wheels slipped into a rabbit hole and the aircraft flipped, killing him instantly.

The All Blacks, who also lost to Wales on that tour, returned home in the summer of 1936 and Eric Tindill, who played at first five-eighth in the England test, had one of the two match balls in his luggage.

RUGBY ODDITIES

Rugby throws up some strange, improbable connections.

There was a story that a New Zealand journalist sat in on the South African team selection meeting in 1937 that astonishingly didn't pick the captain, Philip Nel, for the first test in Wellington. It was never proven or disproven, but that's what the family believes.

This was also the selection meeting that moved the vice-captain, halfback and coming man of rugby, Danie Craven, out to first five-eighth for the occasion.

The journalist was Reg Hornblow, sports editor of the *Evening Post*, who was one of the press corps who tripped around with the Springboks. The story came to light when Hornblow's son, Barry, was talking about an equally improbable story: that the New Zealand Hornblow family was directly related to the American Hornblows, Arthur senior and junior. The senior was a writer and friend of C.S. Forester's and allowed his name to be adapted for Forester's Hornblower novels.

Arthur junior was in the film business and was at one time married to Myrna Loy, an American actress and celebrity of the time whose varied career included the silent movies era.

As with the rugby connection, the novelist connection was also in 1937. That was the year in which the first of Forester's Hornblower novels, *The Happy Return,* was published. It was known as *Beat to Quarters* in the United States.

Arthur senior and Reg Hornblow's grandfathers were brothers apparently, emigrating from England in two different directions.

Barry Hornblow said his father remained in regular touch with Danie Craven after 1937 and even after Reg's death ten years later, Craven continued to write occasionally to his widow Kathleen.

Reg Hornblow, incidentally, in 1939 employed Terry McLean, younger brother of his old travelling companion Gordon (who covered the 1937 tour for the news agency Reuter) and son of the *Post*'s illustrations editor, Jack McLean. Barry Hornblow had no information about his father's role in the selections for the second and third tests when Nel, and sanity, were restored.

It seems not to have been coincidence that without Nel, South Africa lost the first test and, with him, won the next two, giving the Springboks a series win over New Zealand for the first time (the first two series in 1921 and 1928 having been drawn).

While sports editor of the *Evening Post*, Hornblow was said to have played the leading role in establishing the popular Saturday night paper, the *Sports Post*.

FLEETING CAREER

In the days when replacements or substitutions weren't allowed in international rugby, Canterbury wing Don Cobden became known as the twenty-minute All Black. That was the length of time he was on the field in his only test, the first against South Africa in 1937.

Cobden was twice tackled heavily in the match — the first by Springbok prop Cecil Jennings and the second by the man he was marking, wing Dai Williams. According to South African journalist John Sacks: 'Cobden got the ball and tried to pass Williams but the Springbok winger got him by the knees, lifted him off the ground and dumped him so hard that he had to be removed from the field, taking no further part in the game.'

It wasn't just his test career that was fleeting. So was his whole first-class career in New Zealand. Cobden played just eight first-class matches — three for Canterbury, one for the South Island, three All Blacks trials and the test that proved to be his last.

Don Cobden

Soon after the test, Cobden worked his passage on a ship to England and he began playing rugby for the Catford Bridge club in south-east London. He was also accepted for a short-service commission in the Royal Air Force and by the outbreak of war in September 1939, he was a qualified fighter pilot.

On 11 August 1940, his twenty-sixth birthday and almost three years to the day since his only rugby test, Cobden became the first All Black to be killed in action in the Second World War. His squadron was patrolling a convoy in the English Channel when the fighters were attacked by forty German aircraft. His aircraft was seen to crash into the sea soon after midday. His body was washed up on the Belgian coast, recovered by Germans and buried in the Ostende Communal Cemetery.

Cobden had played more first-class matches in Britain than he had in New Zealand. In addition to joining other New Zealanders at the Catford Bridge club, he played for the Royal Air Force and for the Barbarians. One of Cobden's more notable matches was for 'The Empire' against the British Army on 10 February 1940. Among his teammates was Louis Babrow, who had played for South Africa in New Zealand, and Alex Obolensky, the celebrated Russian who scored two tries against the All Blacks in 1936.

The Army included such luminaries as the Welsh pair of Vivian Jenkins and Wilf Wooller plus England's Peter Cranmer (who dropkicked a goal in the 'Obolensky match' against the All Blacks). The Army won 27–9.

FOE AND FRIEND

First, Charles Webb helped beat them. Then he joined them.

Webb, a hard and powerful lock reflecting both his English West Country upbringing and his Royal Marines training, played twelve tests for England in the 1930s. He was known as 'Tankie' because of his size. The last of his tests was in January 1936 when England beat New Zealand in the 'Obolensky match'.

A couple of years later, Webb was posted to the New Zealand division of the Royal Navy, as the terminology of the time had it, and served on board the cruiser, HMS *Leander*. While doing so, he met up with some of his old rugby opponents.

One of the redoubtable All Blacks forwards of the 1930s, Hugh McLean, during the 1935–36 tour had met the secretary of the Barbarians club, Emile de Lissa, and chatted to him about the principles of the club and how it was all for the good of the game. He thought it would work well in New Zealand and when he was home, he raised the idea with his great mate, Ron Bush, a former All Black. He too was enthused and the two set up forming the club, bringing in friends from the Auckland and New Zealand teams.

They first played in Thames in 1937 to give the game a boost there, then did the same in Matamata early in 1938. But the real test was when their distinctive scarlet jerseys with the gambolling lamb on the breast were seen in Auckland for the first time. The occasion was a match against the provincial team at Eden Park.

McLean chose Webb as the first foreigner to play for the Barbarians. Alongside Webb were four who had been on the losing side in the 'Obolensky match' — Pat Caughey, Merv Corner, Bill Hadley and McLean himself. The encounter was a memorable one, the Barbarians winning 45–21 in the sort of sparkling, entertaining rugby that both players and spectators enjoyed most.

By 1941, Webb was serving in the battleship, the *Prince of Wales*, which, as part of the Royal Navy's Z Force, was supposed to show a bit of naval muscle in the waters off Malaya to the advancing Japanese. But it and the battlecruiser *Repulse* were both sunk by Japanese torpedo bombers on 9 December 1941, two days after the attack on Pearl Harbor. Webb found himself in the water and was rescued by a Malay fishing boat; he was eventually captured and spent the rest of the war in a prisoner of war camp.

FORWARD THINKING

One of the defining characteristics of early New Zealand rugby has slipped from human memory. The two-three-two scrum was regarded as the best and quickest way to get the ball to the backs. But it and its attendant wing forward — a sort of extra halfback needed because of the speed the ball went through the scrum — faded away in the 1930s.

As far as can be determined, the last two-three-two scrum to go down in a New Zealand first-class match was on 9 September 1939 when Buller played Fiji in Westport. The Fijians, who were the first team to tour New Zealand unbeaten, packed two-three-two for their first six matches but switched to the now-familiar three-four-one for the last two, which included a win against New Zealand Maori.

Fijians had been coached to pack two-three-two when rugby was introduced there in 1912–13 and had not adapted to a three-man front row when New Zealand did in 1932.

New Zealand dropped the old method because of difficulties when confronting opponents with three-man front rows, especially in South Africa in 1928, and because of continuing criticism, both from New Zealanders and others, of the potential for offside play by the wing forward. The manager of the 1930 British team in New Zealand, James ('Bim') Baxter, in a speech after the team's first tour match in Wanganui, famously labelled the wing forward a cheat.

It's often been written that as a result of Baxter's complaints, the International Rugby Board outlawed the wing forward and made a three-man front row compulsory. But that wasn't so. The New Zealand union's annual meeting in 1932 decided the change itself, though some provincial and club teams continued to persist with the two-three-two because of its efficiency and aid to a faster game.

Northern hemisphere teams generally had a three-two-three formation — hence the origin of the collective phrase, 'back row', for loose forwards — and the present three-four-one was developed in South Africa. It slowly became the norm as countries realised it was more effective for pushing and realised also there was a need for international uniformity.

New Zealanders were reluctant converts. Auckland and Hawke's Bay both advocated at the national union's annual meeting in 1939 for fourteen-a-side teams and two-three-two scrums to be made 'universal'. The NZRFU agreed to submit the remits, but the conference wasn't held because of the Second World War.

The 1924 New Zealand captain, Cliff Porter, continued to argue for a return to two-three-two scrums until he died in 1976. It wasn't until 1954 that the international board altered the law to make a three-man front row compulsory.

FLYING THE FLAG

There seems to be a notion that it's only in the modern era of rugby, when players ply their trade around the globe, that New Zealanders pop up in foreign clubs.

But they've been doing it almost since the beginning of the organised game. One, George Stephenson, of the Wright Stephenson agricultural company, played rugby in England in the nineteenth century and when his club, Manningham, switched to league, he switched too, to become the first New Zealander to play the offshoot game.

New Zealanders who stayed in South Africa after the Boer War early in the twentieth century formed themselves into clubs in Pretoria and Durban and won the local competitions. Similarly, New Zealanders formed their own clubs in Sydney and Melbourne.

One club in England in the 1930s, Catford Bridge in Kent, had so many New Zealanders that it became known as 'London New Zealand'. Among them was Maurice McHugh, who at the time was the New Zealand amateur heavyweight boxing champion. He became an All Black after the Second World War. Another was Don Cobden, the 1937 All Black who had joined the Royal Air Force.

One trial match organised by the club at the start of one season was New Zealanders versus The Rest.

At the close of the first wartime season, 1939–40, the club in its annual report paid tribute to the New Zealanders in its midst. 'Records show that over thirty have played for Catford Bridge during the last two years and they are spoken of as great fellows all,' it said. The club captain said: 'We only hope we shall see more New Zealanders on the resumption of football after the present matter has been settled, as we think they enjoy our company as much as we enjoy theirs.'

One of the reasons so many New Zealanders went to the club, so it was said, was that one of its members worked for the high commission, where most visitors registered when first arriving in the United Kingdom.

While Catford Bridge (now known as Bromley RFC) gained the unofficial name of London New Zealand, there was already an official London New Zealand. It had been formed in 1926 and was based at Aorangi Park, part of the All-England tennis grounds, in Wimbledon. The club had to move in 1981 and is now based at Acton in West London. Over the years, several visiting All Blacks have played for it, including Andy Haden, Doug Rollerson, Paul Sapsford and Terry Morrison. The club has been allowed to retain its black jersey with a silver fern.

THE NEVER-WASSERS

It was the team that never was. New Zealand were supposed to tour South Africa in 1940 and the All Blacks were to have been chosen late in 1939 or early in 1940. But as trials were being played in Wellington, the Second World War began.

The New Zealand Rugby Football Union council met in mid-September and decided to tell South Africa that unless the war was over by 1 January, the tour would have to be called off.

Ted McKenzie of Wairarapa, a remarkable member of a remarkable rugby family, was the sole national selector. Since the war wasn't over by Christmas and since the tour was cancelled, McKenzie's team was never made public. It's not even known if he selected one. If he did, he kept it to himself.

McKenzie died in 1946 and the names he had in mind died with him. There was widespread speculation at the time about who should or should not be in the team and there've been continual comments since about what this player or that player was told, or how a friend of a friend of a friend 'knew' the composition of the team.

McKenzie himself said little publicly.

The 1938 halfback, Charlie Saxton, was often mentioned in speculation as McKenzie's likely choice for captain, but this view may have been influenced,

Charlie Saxton

at least in part, by Saxton's leadership of the 2nd New Zealand Expeditionary Force Kiwis who had such an influence at the end of the war. Saxton was also a possibility as first five-eighth, a position he'd filled in a trial match, rather than halfback.

The All Black and test cricketer, Eric Tindill, who had led one of the trial teams, was also mentioned as a possibility as captain, as was a Wanganui centre, Dave Barton, who led two of the trial teams.

While Ted McKenzie's team can never be known, his brother Norman (himself a national selector at different times) speculated on a test team based on 1939 form (* All Blacks):

Fullback: Jack Taylor (Wellington)*
Three-quarters: Alex Sutherland (Southland), Jack Sullivan (Taranaki),* Tom Morrison (South Canterbury)*
Five-eighths: Pat Grace (Southland), Charlie Saxton (Southland)*
Halfback: Eric Tindill (Wellington)*
No. 8: Ernie Todd (Wellington)
Flankers: 'Snowy' Bowman (Hawke's Bay),* Ron Ward (Southland)*
Locks: Bruce Herron (Southland), Ron King (West Coast)*
Front row: Les George (Southland),* Artie Lambourn (Wellington),* George McDonald (Otago)

Tindill went on to be a test rugby referee and a test cricket umpire; Sullivan and Morrison both became chairmen of the New Zealand union; Saxton, Todd and George served on the NZRFU council.

UNBEATEN TOUR

In the old days of touring, it would have been a common goal to go through unbeaten. But only one team ever managed it. South Africa? The Lions? Australia? No, none of the above.

The only country to send its rugby team to New Zealand and go home without a loss was Fiji. That was an eight-match tour in 1939 and admittedly the Fijians never played the All Blacks, but they did beat New Zealand Maori, Auckland and North Auckland, among others.

Among the players were two future governors-general of Fiji, Ratu Sir George Cakobau, who was captain, and Ratu Sir Panaia Ganilau. All the players were from Fijian clubs except for Imanueli Vosailagi, who was a student at Otago University.

For all the natural quality of the Fijians, much of their success was attributed to their coach, John Bell Kerr Taylor — generally known as 'JBK' — a New Zealander who had played for Auckland and Wellington, was an All Blacks trialist in the 1920s, and was transferred to Fiji in 1930 by the New Zealand Government's works department.

He first coached Fiji on a visit to Tonga in 1934 when they won the first test, lost the second and won the third 30–8. 'It was something about the hard but fatherly way he spurred us on that made us win the third test by a handsome margin,' one of the players, Samu Baravilala, later said.

Stan Dean, the most influential administrator in New Zealand rugby between the wars, managed a national Maori team to Fiji in 1938 and he was so impressed by what he saw, he immediately invited the Fijians to tour the following year.

Taylor, so it was said, had to persuade some of the Fijians to wear boots and as a warm-up to the tour, his chosen XV showed they were ready by beating a Fijian resident Europeans team 78–3.

'The 1939 team took New Zealand by storm,' a history of sixty years of rugby in Fiji said. 'They played attractive unorthodox football at great speed and with fine handling and deadly tackling.'

By the end of the tour, the Second World War had begun and Taylor stayed in Fiji to command the Fijian forces until he was severely wounded by Japanese bombing. After the war, he took up farming in Northland. He was never forgotten in Fiji. When he died in 1985, the *Fiji Sun* carried a headline: 'Our unbeaten coach dies, 90'.

AMBITION THWARTED

Big Jim Wynyard, an All Black in Britain in 1935–36 and again in Australia in 1938, had been in the thick of the war and intended to see it out. He had, it was said, an ambition to drive a troop carrier down the Unter den Linden, the tree-lined boulevard in central Berlin.

But he got no further than El Alamein in North Africa.

As a lieutenant with the Divisional Cavalry, he was part of the brief campaign in Greece in early 1941 and went from there to Crete, where he had his lower jaw shattered by a bullet. He distinguished himself on Crete by several times rescuing men under fire and a colleague once said of him: 'If only there'd been another officer present to verify that bravery, Jim would have won the VC.'

Wynyard recovered from the jaw wound to be promoted to captain and second in command of the regiment, only to be killed in 'Operation Supercharge', the second phase of one of the crucial turning points of the war, the Battle of El Alamein, in October–November 1942.

Wynyard was leading his squadron in the wake of an armoured attack by the Royal Wiltshire Yeomanry when, in the words of the official history, the New Zealanders got 'quite a thrashing' from German anti-tank guns. Among the losses was 'the gay and gallant Jim Wynyard. Poor Jim: he never lived to achieve his ambition of driving a carrier down the Unter den Linden,' the history said.

Wynyard came of fine rugby stock. Three of his uncles, 'Tabby', 'Pie' and 'Sherry', had been members of the pioneering 1888–89 Native team's odyssey through Britain, Australia and New Zealand and 'Tabby' (actually, William Thomas Wynyard) had been a member of the first official New Zealand team in 1893 that was captained by another of the Natives, Tom Ellison.

Wynyard became, at twenty, the youngest member of the 1935–36 All Blacks in Britain. He played in eight of the tour matches and test five-eighth Eric Tindill wrote of him: 'Wynyard is an improving forward of whom more will be heard.'

He toured Australia in 1938 and played in trials in 1939, leading to a belief that he was in line to be chosen for the tour of South Africa in 1940 that did not eventuate. The war came and instead of playing in South Africa, his next rugby was at the other end of the continent when he played in services matches for his regiment and the 2nd New Zealand Expeditionary Force.

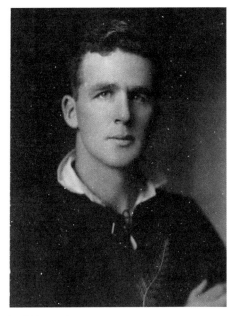

Jim Wynyard

OUR MEN IN LONDON

As difficult as it may be to comprehend these days, the New Zealand union and several provincial unions used to have representatives on the Rugby Football Union, the body that runs English rugby.

For sixty or so years, New Zealand (and Australia and South Africa; not to mention France, which had to wait another thirty years) was not allowed a say in world rugby administration so it was represented on the RFU. So too were some provincial unions and the occasional club (Wellington FC). The NZRFU had two representatives as its men in London from its inception in 1892 until 1949 when the NZRFU (and South Africa and the newly formed Australian RU) finally became members of the International Rugby Board.

The first of the delegates was Charles Frederick Wray Bury Palliser, born of tea planters in Ceylon whose family could claim direct links back to William the Conqueror. He joined the New Zealand civil service in 1873 and had various roles before being dispatched to London as auditor to the New Zealand Government in London and secretary to the agent-general (high commissioner from 1907). Palliser and the agent-general, William Pember Reeves (who played for Canterbury), plus Otago's man on the RFU, Sam Sleigh, were the key figures in the RFU agreeing to New Zealand touring in 1905–06. (Sleigh had managed, and underwritten the cost of, the first New Zealand tour of Australia in 1884.)

Palliser then for the next few years was the man in the middle as the Scottish union complained about the All Blacks being paid and about the RFU agreeing to tour arrangements without first consulting Scotland. Palliser retired to Cornwall in 1916 and died in 1934.

His replacement as the NZRFU man in London was a Wanganui solicitor, Cecil James Wray, who had been in the First XV and First XI at Wanganui Collegiate. He moved to England to work in 1913 and took over his rugby role in the 1919–20 season. He was as influential in his way for the 1924–25 tour as Palliser had been for 1905–06.

Both Palliser and Wray seemed to have been unofficial ambassadors for the many New Zealanders in Britain during and between the wars. There was a story about Wray, then seventy-four, leading an RNZAF team in a haka before a game against the Welsh Guards in 1942. The High Commissioner, Londoner Bill Jordan, shouted 'Remember 1905!' as the air force boys ran out.

DECORATED MINISTER

A war hero, an ordained minister and a rugby fanatic all rolled into one — that was Keith Elliott, once described as an 'honest mix of toughness, hard drinking and earnest praying'.

Elliott won a Victoria Cross for leading a bayonet charge against machine gunners in the Western Desert in 1942, one of just two representative rugby players from New Zealand to be given the ultimate award for bravery (the other was Billy Hardham from the turn-of-the-century Boer War).

When Counties played Wairarapa-Bush in Pukekohe in 1987, the match programme included some reminiscences from Elliott, who was in town for another reason — to officiate at the wedding of recently retired All Blacks captain Andy Dalton and Phillipa Bramwell.

He recalled his days at Feilding Agricultural High School, which had been opened in 1922 with Leonard John Wild as principal. Two of Wild's sons were Sir Richard Wild, the ninth Chief Justice of New Zealand, who played for Wellington

Keith Elliott VC

and New Zealand Universities, and administrator Peter Wild, most noted for managing the Juniors in their 1973 win against the All Blacks.

In 1933 the seventeen-year-old Elliott was in what he said L.J. Wild had termed 'Finlay's Famous Fifteen', captained by future All Black Jack Finlay. His place in the team was, Elliott wrote, his only claim to fame in the rugby world, although he played for Bush thirteen times between 1938 and 1953 (when aged thirty-seven) and played for the Centurions in 1951. He eventually had to give up rugby, he said, because his wife burnt his boots, 'otherwise I would still be playing'.

Elliott said the Bush side was never able to train together because of poor transport and the distance players had to travel. 'We were only farmer-fit, hard-working, raw bone, brainless, rugby fanatics . . . in the winter months the cows were turned out and rugby turned in. There were . . . no showers, perhaps a cow trough or dam to wash in after the game . . .'

Lack of comparative match fitness aside, Elliott said, 'I believe the Bush players with whom I played were much tougher men than we have today because of the extremely hard work they were engaged in.'

Elliott also played battalion rugby during the war and was described by Paul Donoghue, the leading rugby figure of the 22nd Battalion and its chronicler, as a terrific tackler with 'plenty of guts'.

Elliott began training for the Church of England priesthood in 1946 and was ordained in 1948.

ON ACTIVE SERVICE

The last person to emerge from the tunnel in the Great Escape in 1944 at Stalag Luft III in Germany before it was discovered was a New Zealand fighter pilot, Michael Moray Shand. He was the seventy-sixth out and ran for the trees when a startled guard saw Shand's mate, Leonard Trent VC, emerging from the ground.

'I knew we had been rumbled,' Shand recalled years later. 'I don't think the goon knew what was going on either as we all froze. The minute he looked away, I made a run for the woods. That was it. I was out.'

Shand was eventually caught by two railway workers after four days on the run and returned to the camp. Fifty other escapers were rounded up by the Gestapo and shot dead. The story was told in the Paul Brickhill book and the 1963 film, *The Great Escape*.

Shand, who died in 2007, aged ninety-two, had been a member of the successful Nelson College First XV in 1932, whose members showed a high level of commitment to service in the Second World War.

The captain, Jack Stewart, was killed when the Lancaster bomber he was piloting was shot down over France in July 1942. Two of his teammates were also air deaths. Another was in the army and killed in action in Tunisia in 1943.

Of the sixteen players listed in the First XV of that year, twelve served in some capacity during the Second World War. The sixteen who played for Nelson College's First XV in 1932 were:

Jack Graham Stewart, captain, pilot officer, killed on air operations, Germany, July 1942

Clifford Osgood Field, squadron leader, RNZAF

Ralph Kennett Karston, flight lieutenant, RNZAF

Ian Ormonde Stace (who toured Japan with the New Zealand Universities team in 1936), navigator, RNZAF

Norman John Rowe, sergeant-pilot, killed on air operations, September 1942. (Rowe was captain of a Wellington bomber brought down over Germany, killing all five on board)

David Ewing McArthur, dentist

Robert Tannahill Watson, New Zealand Medical Corps, 2nd New Zealand Expeditionary Force

William Arthur Dee, Royal Navy

Le Clerc Stewart Latter, farmer

Michael Moray Shand DFC, flight lieutenant, RAF

Ray Hugh Miller Craighead, RNZAF

Donald Robert Fraser, sergeant, 2nd NZEF, killed in action, Tunisia 1943

Charles Lennox Henderson

Bernard George Benjamin Overton, staff sergeant, 2nd NZEF

Edwin Boyd Boyd-Wilson, dentist

John Edward Fuller, sergeant pilot, killed in air accident, 1940. (Fuller was an air gunner on a Wellington bomber that crashed in the Bristol Channel while on a training flight)

Leonard Trent, who followed Shand out of the tunnel, also went to Nelson College. He won a Victoria Cross for 'cool, unflinching devotion to duty' while leading a flight of Ventura bombers in a raid on a power station in Amsterdam.

THE BOOK

At the end of the Second World War, New Zealand and South African soldiers produced one of rugby's rarest books. Or, rather, produced two of rugby's rarest books — the first a South African version and the second, a New Zealand reply. They were simply called *The Book*.

The title wasn't because the soldiers couldn't think of anything else. The phrase, 'it's in the book', kept coming up when soldiers from the two rugby-loving countries ran into each other in North Africa or Italy. It's believed to have had its origin with a reference to the 1937 South African tour of New Zealand, the series the Springboks won. Whenever a New Zealander would query the outcome, the answer would be, 'It's in the book!'

After the fighting in Italy had ended in 1945, the word became the deed. A noted Cape Town artist among the troops, Richard ('Ginger') Townley Johnson, illustrated *The Book* showing befuddled-looking New Zealanders being instructed by an Afrikaner-looking man with the South African 6th Division's crest on his breast. And it carried lines such as: 'And the Springbok did verily overpower and smite the Kiwi tribesmen, saying to them "Go ye to the men of Iti land and first practice the art of rugby with them, learning from the great and wise script which is called De Book".'

The New Zealand troops responded in kind with the assistance of official war artist Peter McIntyre. A similar-looking pamphlet was produced, with a Kiwi instructor on the front and the words: 'THIS is the book!' And within was contained the response: 'Lo! The teams moved on the face of the field and there were Kiwis crying in the scrum, "Suffer little Springboks and come unto us and we shall teach you the Laws of the Book".'

The South African version made its first appearance as a programme for a match between the 2nd New Zealand Expeditionary Force and the 6th South African Armoured Division at Rapallo on the Italian Riviera south of Genoa on 10 November 1945. The New Zealand rejoinder, 'THIS is The Book', served as the programme for a return match in Florence nine days later.

Both books were printed on ordinary paper and without covers or proper binding. As a result, they were not built to last and are now among the rarest rugby publications. Journalist and broadcaster Wallie Ingram described *The Book* (whichever version it was) as being 'one of the most treasured souvenirs of the Italian campaign and no lucky Springbok or Kiwi who managed to secure a copy will ever be persuaded to part with it'.

THE GENERAL'S TEAM

When the first of the New Zealand troops arrived in Egypt in January 1940 at the start of the Second World War, the general officer commanding the 2nd New Zealand Expeditionary Force, Major-General Bernard Freyberg, invited one of his captains, Allan Andrews, to his Cairo flat for tea.

Both were well-known New Zealand sporting men: Freyberg for rugby and for swimming, and Andrews for famously turning down a chance in 1934 of being an All Black — he put university studies first.

'After dinner and over a brandy and cigars,' Andrews recalled, 'he first propounded his vision of a 2NZEF rugby team touring the UK after the war, as happened in 1919.'

In January of 1940, there was still more than five years of war to come. In those five years, the New Zealand army men under Freyberg's command were to fight in Greece, Crete, North Africa and Italy. Many would die, many were to be taken prisoner. 'Right throughout the war the General, even in the black days when the Division was being mauled and hammered,' Andrews wrote, 'never lost sight of his great ambition to see his rugby team march through the British Isles after the war playing rugby of a quality that would be an inspiration to all rugby players who either played against the Kiwis or watched them play.'

On 13 May 1943 near Enfidaville in north-eastern Tunisia, Freyberg waited to accept the surrender of the senior German and Italian commanders in North Africa. While waiting, Andrews recalled, the conversation went back to rugby. 'It became clear to me that a successful 2NZEF rugby team playing rugby of a high standard was almost as important to the General as winning the war.'

The team became known as the Kiwis and was chosen after trials in Austria and Margate. From late October 1945, when they made their debut against Swansea, until early August 1946, they played thirty-eight matches in the British Isles and New Zealand, and they won thirty-two of them, drew three and lost three. They scored nearly three times as many points as their opponents. But it was not a tour whose qualities could be illuminated by statistics. It was the manner of the Kiwis' play rather than their win-loss ratio that attracted attention wherever they went.

When the Kiwis were chosen, Saxton was the only All Black. Sixteen more went on to play for New Zealand, some of them such as Bob Scott being regarded as among the best in their positions; Fred Allen captained the All Blacks in the tests of the 1940s but gained a greater fame as a coach of Auckland during the Ranfurly Shield era of the 1960s and an unbeaten coach of the All Blacks.

The Kiwis stand easy outside the gates of Buckingham Palace after meeting the King and Queen.

THE BIG GAME

Rugby has never just been about a game. Its appeal is much wider than a piece of ground measuring 120 metres or so by about half that. It's about rivalries not between players but between clubs and geographical areas; between sections of society; between provinces. And those rivalries are set aside for the greater good of the national team. Rugby has a layered loyalty.

Club rugby has always been at the core of the game, the heart that pumps lifeblood to the rest. Its appeal was captured most eloquently in a short story published soon after the Second World War by a schoolteacher, Alec Pickard, who wrote under the name of A.P. Gaskell.

He called the story 'The Big Game' and it quickly achieved a secure place among the classics of New Zealand literature. It is most often described as being about a 1936 club rugby match in Dunedin between University and Southern. It was the match that would decide that year's premiership. It is and it isn't. The story ends with the kick-off and the narrator (Pickard, who was a Varsity lock in the game) saying, 'The game at last!'

The story is about the week's build-up to the match and is about the culture of the time and how the whole city, it seemed, was anticipating and on edge about the pending match: the middle-class boys from the Varsity against the working-class boys from South Dunedin; students against railway workers and labourers; and, unspoken in the story but implicit, 'old' Vic Cavanagh coaching University and his son, 'Young Vic', coaching Southern. (The two, father and son, coached Otago, then young Cavanagh famously went on to coach Otago through a Ranfurly Shield era in the 1940s.)

The intensity was summed up by Pickard as he sat in the Carisbrook dressing room after the previous week's match: 'I've just been thinking, here we are just after slogging through one hard game and before we're off the ground even, everyone wants to play next week's game with us. Why can't they give us a spell?'

Pickard (1913–2006) was a schoolteacher all his working life but a writer of short stories for only a small part of it; the literary flow stopped in the early

1950s. 'I stopped possibly because I felt I had said all I had to say, which is probably not true but makes a good answer for myself,' he once told a radio interviewer.

A YEAR TO FORGET

More than most of the words, a full-page cartoon in 1949 summed up New Zealand rugby's fervent hope that the All Blacks in South Africa would win the series there for the first time and help wipe out the bitter memories of the series loss at home against the Springboks in 1937.

Drawn by artist Neville Colvin, it graced the front page of the *Sports Post*, the Saturday night edition of the Wellington daily, the *Evening Post*. It showed an ageing man, clad in pyjamas and dressing gown and with an unlit pipe protruding from his mouth, sitting on the edge of a seat by one of those old valve radios that used to stand on the floor. Teapot and two-bar heater sit at his slippered feet. Behind him, unseen, is a burglar, his haul forgotten in a bag on the floor behind him, similarly engrossed in what the voice coming over the air waves would have to say.

On the wall are photos of past glories; on the radio are books, *With the 1905 All Blacks* and *Great Names in Rugby*; a signed photo of Billy Wallace sits alongside. A newspaper lies on the floor, its one headline exposed: 'All set for the test'.

It was published on Saturday, 16 July, the day of the first test in Cape Town. Colvin's image could have been any household in New Zealand on that winter's day. People rising in the dead of night, early in the morning on the 17th, to listen to the crackling, fading radio commentary by Winston McCarthy from far-off Newlands.

Such was the hope, such was the expectation, that the All Blacks of 1949 would go where no All Blacks team had gone before: victory against South Africa. The first series in 1921 in New Zealand had been drawn, so too the second series in South Africa in 1928. The 1937 series of three tests was South

Africa's by two tests to one. Now it was New Zealand's turn.

But no. Not only did the All Blacks, as history grimly records, lose the first test 15–11, but they lost the second as well. And the third. And the fourth. Four tests. Four losses. The hope that turned into despair was underlined by two other tests at home, played by a 'third' New Zealand team against Australia, both lost. A year that began full of promise and confidence ended in introspection and shattering disappointment.

HEAD-ON CRASH

The All Blacks of 1949 would have taken a while to put Rhodesia out of their minds. It was the crown colony of Southern Rhodesia then, not the Zimbabwe it later became, and for rugby purposes was a province of South Africa.

They went there for the fourteenth and fifteenth games of their tour of twenty-five matches, between Transvaal in Johannesburg and Northern Transvaal in Pretoria. It was all by train — about 800 km to Bulawayo for the first match (lost 10–8) and another 450 km to Salisbury for the second (drew 3–3). Five hours into the 1000-km rail journey back south to Pretoria, the steam locomotive hauling their train crashed head on into a mail train. Both drivers had realised they were on an inevitable collision course and were able to slow enough to minimise the impact.

But even so, the two locomotives were locked together in a tangle of steel, one carriage telescoped and another flung sideways down an embankment. It happened at about two in the morning and most on the train would have been sleeping. The All Blacks were flung out of their bunks, but none was seriously hurt. The lock, Charlie Willocks, later reported a sore shoulder and that was enough to keep him out of the second test.

Several of the other passengers were injured and an African driver's assistant died not long after the collision. He'd been trapped in the locomotive and was scalded by steam. Among those trying to help him was the All Blacks centre, Ron Elvidge, who was in the last year of his medical studies. The crash

The aftermath (top) and Des Christian and Fred Allen while waiting for a replacement train.

remained etched on Elvidge's mind, even when he was into his nineties and affected by dementia. 'Ah yes, the poor native chap,' he responded when asked in 2017 about the crash.

One of the South African journalists following the tour, C.J. Ferreira, thought when he was woken by the crash that the locomotive must have hit an elephant. He joined rescuers at the front of the train, doing what they could. 'Ron really put up a magnificent show that night,' Ferreira wrote. 'He was helping all over the show and he tried his utmost to free the trapped native.'

A relief train eventually picked up the weary players and they finally got to Pretoria on the Wednesday morning, about eighty hours after leaving Salisbury. They had been trying to sleep on trains for eight nights out of eleven.

The driver of the All Blacks' train was charged with culpable homicide and acquitted. The court instead censured Rhodesian Railways for making its drivers work dangerously long hours.

A SPORTING LIFE

Faced with the choice of banking a cheque for several thousand pounds to play league or fighting in a war, most people would take the money. But not Ernie Hills, an Aucklander who played for Australia against the British Isles in 1950.

His was an unusual story, seldom told.

Hills was born in Manurewa, grew up in Mangere and went to Otahuhu College, where he showed an aptitude for a variety of sports. Most of all, he was fast and, when he was nineteen, decided to go to Sydney to see if he could get a bit more speed in his legs so he'd be picked for the Empire Games in Auckland in 1950.

He fell in with a coach who gave him the chance to take up the lucrative professional running circuit in Victoria, but he wanted to give running for New Zealand a chance first. He returned home, failed to be selected, so went to Melbourne.

He ran in pro races over the 1949–50 summer and as winter approached, he started playing for the Melbourne rugby club as a wing. His speed got him noticed, he was selected for Victoria and in a match against Queensland, the national selectors thought they saw enough to put him into the Australian team to play the British Isles in two tests. The Wallabies were thumped in the first test, but Hills must have done enough because he was retained for the second, when the Wallabies were thumped again.

On the morning after the second test, Hills told Greymouth-born Canberra journalist Robert Messenger in 2019, he was made a £4000 offer to join Halifax in the English league.

But Hills' brother Jack back in Auckland had an alternative. He rang Ernie — who was nicknamed 'Nigger' during his career — and said he'd signed up to go with the New Zealand forces to the war in Korea. That was enough for Ernie. He tried to sign up in Melbourne, couldn't, so scooted back across the Tasman to get into Kayforce.

He served 1951–53 and also played some rugby, being the only international in a New Zealand Kayforce team that toured Japan in 1952 and played two 'tests' against All-Japan. From wearing the green of Australia two years before, Hills now found himself in the more appropriate black of his own country.

He returned to Melbourne after the war, moved to Sydney and saw out his unusual sporting life by playing a couple of seasons for Western Suburbs in the Australian Rugby League.

'OUR OWN'

When Canterbury headed south to challenge Otago for the Ranfurly Shield in 1950, few people gave Canterbury much of a chance.

After all, Otago had won nineteen shield matches in succession — a successful challenge against Southland in 1947 and eighteen defences. The shield had been held by either Otago or Southland since 1935. It seemed anchored in the south.

Furthermore, Otago beat Southland 22–3 in the first defence of 1950 and a week later, Southland beat Canterbury 25–8 in Invercargill. Canterbury had a challenge against Otago on the following Wednesday and such was the lack of expectation in Christchurch, the morning paper, the *Press,* chose not to send its main rugby writer, Jack Mullins, to Dunedin. It would just take the *Otago Daily Times* coverage supplied through the New Zealand Press Association, it decided.

Meanwhile, a promising young Canterbury wing, Jim Kennedy, had been injured in the Invercargill game and a replacement, Barry Simpson, was put on the express train south. Simpson worked as a general reporter at the *Press* and had to get the permission of the editor for a couple of days off.

Since Simpson was there, the *Press* sports editor reasoned, he could also write about it. His initial brief was to provide 500 words on an expected loss.

But then the unthinkable happened. Canterbury beat Otago 8–0, first five-eighth Peter Kearney and Tommy Lynch each scoring tries, with Kearney converting one of them.

No sooner showered and changed, Simpson received a telegram from the *Press* increasing its demand ten-fold for 5000 words on Canterbury's first shield win in fifteen years.

Simpson duly obliged and the *Press* the next day was able to run the proud byline, 'From Our Own Reporter'.

As any back should, Simpson gave most of the credit for the win to the Canterbury forwards: 'Canterbury's win was attributable to the magnificent play of its forwards. Time after time the Canterbury forwards swept upfield in foot rushes that had Otago defending desperately.'

Canterbury's reign was brief. They lost the shield in the first challenge to Wairarapa, then South Canterbury took it to Timaru and in their first defence, lost it to North Auckland.

Simpson had three more games in 1950 and one each in 1951 and 1952. He's probably the only reporter to have played in a shield match, then written about it. The Taranaki halfback, Roger Urbahn, may have reported games in which he played while he worked for the *Taranaki Daily News*, but there's been no mention of him covering his own shield games.

JARDEN'S YEAR

Every so often a tour was remembered not so much for the results or what the team did collectively, but for the achievements of an individual. This was the case when the All Blacks went to Australia in 1951 and regained the Bledisloe Cup.

The three tests and all other ten matches were won, but this was the year of Ron Jarden, the Wellington wing, twenty-one years old, who dominated rugby talk on both sides of the Tasman. Wellingtonians had been talking about him since 1949 when he first played first-class rugby as a nineteen-year-old. He gained some national attention in 1950 when he played for the North Island, although all that was but an overture to the main event of 1951.

Jarden toured Australia with the New Zealand Universities team and such was his impact there that the national selectors couldn't have pondered for long about who their main left wing would be. He and the Auckland five-eighth, John Tanner, were both still in Australia with the universities team when the All Blacks touring squad was named.

Jarden's impact was immediate and immense. He scored a try in his first match, against New South Wales, his second match was his test debut and in his third scored six tries against Central West at Parkes. In the following match

Ron Jarden

against an Australian XV in Melbourne, he scored another five. His next match was the second test when he scored two tries, the first of them within thirty seconds of the start. He scored again against Queensland and by the end of the tour had a total of eighty-eight points from fifteen tries, seventeen conversions and three penalty goals — all from six matches. He had to miss the third test because of injury.

Jarden's thirty-eight points at Parkes was a record tally for an All Black in a game, beating the twenty-eight scored by Billy Wallace against Devon in 1905. When the All Blacks arrived in Melbourne for their next match, against an Australian XV, a telegram was waiting for Jarden. It was from Wallace: 'Heartiest congratulations. Keep up the good work.'

Jarden played another thirteen tests — for a total tally of seven tries, six conversions and three penalty goals — before a surprise retirement at the age of twenty-seven to concentrate on becoming a sharebroker. In his last series, against South Africa in 1956, he scored the All Blacks' only try for a win in the first test.

A TRIO OF CAPTAINS

A Roman Catholic priest watched the All Blacks play Ulster in Belfast in 1953 with more than just rugby interest. Brother Murphy, originally from Cork, had spent thirty years teaching in New Zealand and among his pupils at St Kevin's College in Oamaru had been two of the players, Kevin Skinner and Bill McCaw.

Murphy, of the Congregation of Christian Brothers, in 1953 was the superior at Lake Glen Students' Hostel in Andersonstown in the west of Belfast, and he called by the team's hotel to say hello. The priest and the two All Blacks — who had both been in the St Kevin's First XV in 1944 — spent the day together on the day before the game, Murphy showing the players the sights.

Murphy had taught Skinner and McCaw in 1944 and left New Zealand in 1948. 'He's a fine man,' Skinner said of his former teacher. 'They're grand boys,' Murphy said of his former pupils.

Murphy missed seeing another St Kevin's old boy, the captain, Bob Stuart, who had driven about a 300-km round trip from Belfast to Letterkenny in County Donegal to see a great-uncle, Bill Kearney, who had a farm outside the town. (That was the second connection between Letterkenny and an All Blacks captain. The 1905–06 captain, Dave Gallaher, was born at Ramelton about 20 km away and the Letterkenny club has claimed him as one of its own and has renamed its ground Dave Gallaher Park.)

The three St Kevin's old boys may also have created a unique record on tour because Skinner and McCaw captained the All Blacks in tour matches, as of course did Stuart. McCaw was leader against the North of Scotland and Skinner, who'd captained the All Blacks against Australia in 1952, led the team on four occasions.

There have been some instances of two from the same school captaining the All Blacks but not three, and not all three on the same tour. Even more remarkably, St Kevin's at that stage had produced only four All Blacks, the other being Jim Kearney of 1947 and 1949. The school later gained another three — Frank McAtamney (1956), Tom Coughlan (1958) and Kevin Laidlaw (1960).

Skinner and McCaw, like Stuart, came from Irish stock. Skinner had a grandmother named O'Sullivan, who came from Cork, but he didn't think he had any living relatives there. The same applied to McCaw, whose antecedents were also from Munster.

(Jim Kearney appears not to have been related to the Kearney side of Bob Stuart's family.)

UP, UP AND AWAY

Modern rugby players are as familiar with aircraft and flying as they are with their own cars. But there was a day when flying was a novelty.

All Blacks went aloft in aeroplanes for the first time, as All Blacks anyway, on 16 November 1924 at Croydon in South London. Imperial Airways, a forerunner of BOAC and British Airways, made three aircraft available and players went in groups on sightseeing trips of about half an hour. Seating was in cane chairs and the Canterbury lock, Read Masters, described the aircraft cabin as a glorified railway saloon. They went up about 2000 feet and flew at about 80 to 90 miles an hour. They went as far north as the Tower of London and the docks, and Masters said they went over Crystal Palace three times, though their view was sometimes hindered by fog.

A month after this joyriding, Imperial Airways had its first fatal crash when one of its aircraft crashed on take-off from Croydon, killing all eight on board.

The All Blacks had been scheduled to fly across the Channel for their games in France but instead went by train and ship, mainly because of weight.

The tour of Australia in 1951 was the first time the team flew on an international tour. Their trans-Tasman conveyance was a Solent flying boat which took seven hours fifteen minutes to make the trip from Evans Bay in Wellington to Rose Bay in Sydney. This was the tour on which New Zealand regained the Bledisloe Cup after losing it in 1949. Regaining it, that is, after a search for it revealed it to be lying in a Melbourne warehouse among disused tourism props such as cellophane mountains and cardboard trees. The first test in Sydney was also played for the little-known Commonwealth Jubilee Cup, a handsome-looking trophy that marked fifty years of Australian federation.

The first time the All Blacks flew to the northern hemisphere was the long tour in 1953–54. Long-haul flights in those days really did mean long haul. The journey began, as in 1951, at Evans Bay in Wellington for the first leg to Sydney. Then an overnight flight to Darwin. After a two-hour stop, the next leg was to Singapore. Two nights were spent there, then another flight to

Calcutta (now Kolkata). The next leg was supposed to be overnight to Beirut, but a mechanical fault had them land at Basra on the Arabian Gulf for a night, then on to Beirut. The journey continued to Zurich with a refuelling stop at Rome, then finally a last flight to London, five days after leaving Wellington.

GREAT SCOTT

Bob Scott was generally regarded as one of the best New Zealand fullbacks of the amateur era, ranking with Billy Wallace (when he wasn't on the wing), George Nepia and Don Clarke.

Scott was an attacking fullback when it wasn't fashionable to be so, and was encouraged in this by Charlie Saxton, his captain in the 2nd NZEF Kiwis after the war. The tour made Scott's name, but he could have been left out because he'd played league before the war. The NZEF commander, Bernard Freyberg, who came up with the idea of the Kiwis' tour, learnt late in the war that selectors were worried about choosing Scott and the prop, John Simpson, because of their league backgrounds.

'If they're good enough, pick them,' Freyberg was reputed to have said.

(The army Kiwis, like the New Zealand Services teams in the United Kingdom and the army team that won the King's Cup in 1919, were chosen, administered and financed within the services; none had anything to do with the New Zealand Rugby Football Union.)

Scott was a straightforward choice for the All Blacks after the war for the first two series against Australia, to tour South Africa in 1949 and play in each of the four tests in 1950 against the British Isles.

He broke down in tears and apologised to his teammates for missed attempts at goal during the four-nil loss in South Africa, but captain Fred Allen and others assured him the losses were due to reasons other than goal-kicking. Allen and Scott were firm friends and together represented New Zealand in a wreath-laying at the Menin Gate at Ypres on the ninetieth anniversary of the Passchendaele battle in 2007.

Scott was talked out of retirement so he could play on the 1953–54 British tour and was even asked to come out of retirement for the 1956 series against South Africa, but on this occasion, declined. This allowed room for Don Clarke's debut in the third test in Christchurch.

Scott's party trick was to kick goals with bare feet which he did most famously to win a bet with Harold Day, a 1920s England wing working as a journalist, in Eastbourne in 1953 and repeated on many occasions on New Zealand football grounds.

Scott met his future wife Irene in England during the war but returned home with the Kiwis ahead of her. When he was chosen to play against Australia, he cabled her and told her proudly he'd been chosen for the All Blacks.

'What are All Blacks?' Irene responded.

Bob Scott shows his style while playing for the Kiwis against British Combined Services in Hamburg.

TRAIN DISASTERS

When something of significance happens in New Zealand, invariably there's a rugby connection.

Take the country's worst rail disaster, for example, when the Wellington–Auckland express plunged into a river at Tangiwai on Christmas Eve 1953, with the loss of 151 lives. Two of the rescuers received the George Medal for bravery — Cyril Ellis, who tried to flag the train down before it steamed on to the broken bridge, and John Holman who, with Ellis, stood up to his chest in floodwaters and helped twenty-one people out of one of the doomed carriages.

Holman, it turned out, had moved to New Zealand the previous year with his wife Delia. They'd lived in Harrow near London and Holman had played rugby for the Wasps club. Both the club and the local paper, the *Harrow Observer and Gazette*, recorded Holman's role and his reaction to receiving the highest civilian award for gallantry. He and Delia had continued on holiday and authorities couldn't find him to tell him so he read about the award in a paper. 'By God, dear,' he was reported to have said to his wife, 'I've won the George Medal.' Wasps produced a small book in 1967 to mark the club's centenary and included a page that listed club members who had been decorated for gallantry in the Second World War. The last paragraph read: 'J.W. Holman was awarded the GM for gallantry in a train disaster in New Zealand, Christmas 1953.' A brother, William, had also played for Wasps and was killed in action in Korea, two days after being made a member of the Order of the British Empire (MBE, military division).

Rugby also had a role in the third-worst railway disaster when the Auckland–Wellington express ran into a slip at Ongarue in King Country in 1923, killing seventeen and injuring twenty-eight. Among the passengers was the national Maori team, which had lost to Auckland two days earlier and was on its way to Wanganui for the next match. A doctor on board, David Bathgate, wrote later about the confusion, the chaos and agonising screaming in the night, lit only by the glow from the overturned locomotive firebox. The Maori joined other unhurt passengers in helping and doing what they could and were 'a wonderful help', according to the doctor. A day after the crash, the Maori beat Wanganui 15–8.

PROP TO THE RESCUE

Much has been written about the recall of prop Kevin Skinner to the New Zealand front row for the third and fourth tests against South Africa in the tumultuous 1956 series. The All Blacks won the first test, but lost a prop, Mark Irwin. They lost the second test and lost another prop, Frank McAtamney.

The country was in crisis. Skinner had played eighteen tests and was reckoned to be one of the best props New Zealand had had. But he'd retired after the 1953–54 northern hemisphere tour. The New Zealand union, obsessed with beating South Africa, enticed him back. Skinner recalled that he arrived in Christchurch for the third test and was alarmed to hear hard men of the stature of Bob Duff and 'Tiny' White saying they were being intimidated by the Springboks.

Skinner always reckoned that the stories about what happened next were exaggerated and painted him as an avenging Darth Vader; the fact he'd been a national heavyweight boxing champion was usually slipped into the stories.

What happened was prosaic by the standards of rugby at the time. As Skinner related in a 'this is what really happened' speech, the first issue was with one of the South African props, Chris Koch, advancing on to the New Zealand side in lineouts. The first time he did it in Christchurch, Skinner told him that would be the last time. Koch tried it again; Skinner hit him. There was no further trouble in the lineouts.

What happened in the scrums was simply told. Ian Clarke had been marking the biggest South Africa tighthead, Jaap Bekker, in the first half. Out on the field at halftime, Clarke told Skinner he wouldn't mind a swap. So they swapped. 'Bekker started trying to pop me, dropping his shoulder and generally making a nuisance of himself. I conveyed my sentiments to Jaap, and we had a bit of a dust-up. Two or three scrums later, the ref had a word to the captains. There was no further trouble.'

New Zealand won the third test 17–10 and clinched the series with an 11–5 win in the fourth.

Skinner got so tired of the exaggerated stories which were written for months, even years, afterwards, he once wrote to the editor of the *Auckland Star* asking him to find some other news.

What's not often been related in the aftermath was that a week after the fourth test, Skinner and his two protagonists, Koch and Bekker, were teammates for the Barbarians against a Coronation Shield district team. Forty thousand showed up at Eden Park to see the combined team beat the Barbarians 25–18.

Kevin Skinner swigs lemonade after the fourth test against South Africa. That's flanker Bill Clark in the souvenired jersey.

MATCH FIXING?

It's hard to imagine a politician telling a rugby team before an important match to take it easy. It's even harder for any of the players to take any such suggestion seriously.

But that was what, according to one of the players, happened before the South Africans thumped the national Maori team 37–0 at Eden Park in 1956.

The Maori match was the third-last on that most dramatic of tours and followed losses by the Springboks in the third test and against New Zealand Universities. The Maori team included two who had played in the third test, captain Bill Gray and lock Stan Hill, plus another two who were in the test reserves, Pat Walsh and Keith Davis.

Maori flocked to Eden Park from around the country, crammed into their iwi-designated seats, hoping for success against such a formidable foe. But the Maori were a flop. They never scored and the South Africans played, or were allowed to play, their best game of the tour.

Fifty-four years later, the Maori fullback that day, Muru Walters, told a radio host, Willie Jackson, the grandson of an All Black, that before the game, the Maori Affairs Minister, Ernest Corbett, went into the dressing room and told the Maori that for the future of rugby, they must not beat the Springboks. Corbett's view, according to Walters, was that if the Maori won, the All Blacks would not be invited back to South Africa.

Walters told Jackson that the comment 'ripped the guts out of our spirits of our team'.

But Stan Hill had a different memory. He said Corbett wasn't even in the dressing room. Neither had he been at Titirangi, where the Maori had prepared the day before.

So what really happened? Corbett, who stood down from politics the following year and died in 1968, appears never to have said anything publicly about the match. It's unlikely any politician, even then, would have had the gall to tell players to throw a game. What seems more likely is a warning against any incidents, especially of the type in 1921 when the Springboks, both the team and followers, were accused of racism against the Maori. The 1921 match was one of the reasons why South Africa in 1937 did not play a Maori team.

Although by 1956 there was increasing opposition to New Zealand teams going to South Africa without Maori, there was barely a voice raised in protest against the presence of the Springboks in New Zealand.

RENAISSANCE MAN

Pat Vincent was a man of rare distinction among All Blacks. In a purely rugby sense, he was noted for playing just two tests and being captain in both — the first two of the 1956 series against South Africa.

A halfback, he had a long career with Canterbury (102 matches) and led the side through its Ranfurly Shield era of the early 1950s. Vincent had had All Blacks trials since 1951 and been the South Island halfback since 1953, but his selection as captain for the first two South African tests was still something of a surprise.

His fall was as rapid as his rise, being dumped after the South Africans won the second test.

Vincent was a schoolteacher whose wit was as quick as his pass. He was once called upon to cane a boy called Heald. 'You are about to find out,' Vincent told him, 'that time wounds all Healds.' A history teacher, he was talking about the American Revolution to his class, which included a boy called Herd. 'You ought to be sent up in a rocket then you could be the Herd that was shot around the world.' These one-liners were included in a tribute book compiled by a friend, Alan Barley, after Vincent died of asthma-related complications while he was living in the United States.

Vincent had a fascination with America and the Americans. He did a master's degree at the University of California at Berkeley when he'd retired from playing, then eventually settled in San Francisco. He had a rugby

Pat Vincent

involvement there, among other things managing the Californian Grizzlies who toured New Zealand in 1972. He was one of the founding members of the United States Rugby Union, president of the Northern Californian union and coached rugby at St Mary's College at Moraga, inland from San Francisco, and according to the college, so many wanted to play under his tutelage that other sports suffered.

Vincent also wrote two small instruction books, *Rugby Football for Americans*, and *How to Make a Half Back from Nothing*, both displaying his sense of humour.

Vincent was also a noted jazz singer and performed regularly in Christchurch in the 1960s and had a couple of records released, one of them, 'I've Got the World on A String', proving especially popular. He and George Nepia are probably the only individual All Blacks to have made records.

Vincent had been on an Easter tour to Europe with St Mary's and suffered an asthma attack on the flight home. The aircraft landed at Pittsburgh for him to receive specialised care, but it was too late. The college called him a Renaissance man and the rugby ground there is now the Patrick Vincent Memorial Field.

ONE-ARMED

Bob Forsyth, a useful first five-eighth before the Second World War and an accomplished referee after it, had a couple of rare claims to rugby fame.

Forsyth played for Marlborough when in his late teens, signed up with the army and went to war as a gunner with the 38th Field Regiment in the South

Pacific. He was caught up in an explosion at Guadalcanal in the Solomon Islands and lost his right arm.

He returned to Taranaki and took up refereeing, having a distinguished career that encompassed fixtures at all levels, including a Bledisloe Cup test in 1958, Ranfurly Shield matches, national trials and British Isles tour matches. An added cachet was that his test was the only one to be played at the Epsom Showgrounds, Auckland's alternate test venue when improvements were being carried out at Eden Park.

Forsyth also had an unwitting role in the infamous Andy Haden dive in the 1978 test against Wales. He had been in charge of a game between Taranaki and King Country in which Colin Meads was proving to be a bit of a nuisance to Taranaki in lineouts. Coach J.J. Stewart (the 1974–76 All Blacks coach) and lock Ian Eliason hit on the ploy of Eliason falling out of the lineout while shouting, 'Aw, ref!' Forsyth penalised Meads, who later recalled the incident with less glee than did Eliason.

Captain Graham Mourie told the story that when Eliason, watching the 1978 test on television from his dairy farm, saw Haden's unsuccessful attempt to milk a penalty, he shouted to his wife Ngaire and anyone in hearing distance, 'That's my trick!'

Strangely enough, Forsyth was not the only one-armed man to referee a test match.

William Simeon Bailey Chapman, born in 1898, enlisted in the Cyclist Corps of the Australian Imperial Force in August 1915. He later transferred to an infantry battalion and suffered a gunshot wound to his right arm in 1918. He was sent to England where the arm was amputated. He played rugby again after the war but ultimately became a referee. Bill Chapman was in charge of the first and third Bledisloe Cup tests in 1938.

A veterans' newspaper, *Reveille*, said Chapman had so impressed the New Zealand captain, Brushy Mitchell, in the first test that he asked for him for the third. Like Forsyth, the lack of an arm didn't hold Chapman back. He refereed 138 Sydney first-grade matches, including four grand finals.

CLARKE 18, LIONS 17

There were times during the tour by the British Isles in 1959 when players from both sides must have wondered what was going on. Late in the first test in Dunedin, the All Blacks in front, and the capacity crowd at Carisbrook chanted: 'Red, red, red.' And in Auckland for the fourth test, the series already decided and New Zealand leading in the match, the chant came again. 'Red, red, red.'

It may have been a reflection of how enormously popular the Lions were; it may have been just a championing of the underdog. In Dunedin, it may simply have been that the crowd thought the Lions were hard done by.

The Lions did everything but win the first test. They scored four tries, twice as many as they'd scored in any previous match against New Zealand. But they lost because referee Alan Fleury, a 37-year-old accountant, found reason to penalise them twenty-one times (and New Zealand fourteen times). The All Blacks' fullback, Don Clarke, had ten shots at goal and succeeded with six

Don Clarke could run as well as kick: he evades Lions wing Peter Jackson in the first test.

of them, leading to the cruel headline in the sports edition of the Dunedin *Evening Star*: Clarke 18, Lions 17.

The All Blacks were rearranged for the second test; not because of injury but because of dissatisfaction with their performance. It was a much-improved performance, if still not wholly convincing, by New Zealand. Ralph Caulton got two tries on debut and just to prove that he was not just a kicker, Clarke scored after a spectacular dive over the line.

The All Blacks finally established dominance in the third. One writer said they were better by a third than they had been in Dunedin and Wellington.

Despite having lost the test series, the Lions were still seen as a chance when they got to Auckland for the final test. It was a chance they took. The Lions won by scoring three tries to two penalty goals by Don Clarke. Much of the comment during and after the tour centred on the penalties the Lions conceded, especially in the first test, and how New Zealand referees had a different interpretation of the laws than the British and Irish players were used to. The International Rugby Board met at Wairakei during the tour. It was the first time it had met outside the United Kingdom or Ireland and was, therefore, the first time some of its members could see at first hand that rugby was what people made it, not what English people in the late nineteenth century decided it should be. It was also a lesson for the IRB that unlike in England, rugby was the game of the people.

DICK'S DIGIT

A quick trip to the doctor for Dick Conway in 1960 has earned him an enduring niche in rugby lore.

Conway, more often than not known as 'Red', had made a spectacular international debut when he played for New Zealand against the Lions in 1959 and desperately wanted to be chosen for the tour of South Africa in 1960.

But there was a problem. In the summers, he was a softball catcher and one of the occupational hazards of the position was getting the ball in the hand that didn't have a glove. The third finger of his right hand had been

Dick Conway

sprained and then broken by balls which had whacked into it.

The break mended but the finger had a permanent kink and a surgeon told Conway that if he continued to play football, it would break again.

With the prospect of the tour of South Africa, Conway decided to get the digit lopped off. Things happened rapidly for Conway in April 1960.

On the 18th, a Monday, he played in the fourth All Blacks trial. The fifth trial was on the Thursday, the 21st, and the selectors named their team for South Africa that night. It was in the papers the next day. Conway played for his club, Zingari-Richmond, whom he captained, on the Saturday and on the Monday, which was Anzac Day, he had the troublesome finger amputated. A fortnight after that, he assembled in Auckland with the rest of the All Blacks and told the coach, Jack Sullivan, that he'd be as right as rain.

He recalled years later: 'I still could have gone to South Africa with the finger [as it was] but if it had broken again I would have had to go through the whole process again and miss too much footy. So I reckoned getting it taken off was the best option.'

He played in Australia at the start of the tour wearing a protective mitt 'but by the time the tour proper started I was as right as rain'. Conway played in eighteen of the thirty-two tour matches, including three of the four tests, and he played for New Zealand against The Rest in Wellington not long after they arrived home. In a tour summary, he was described as a terrific tackler.

He played for New Zealand again in 1965, again against South Africa, and continued to play first-class rugby until 1968.

SAVIOUR SOURED

An All Black who's probably not all that well known, Des Oliver, might have reflected on the bitter-sweet ironies of life thirty years after his playing career when he was the central figure in a medical controversy.

Oliver was a flanker for Otago while at Medical School and on the strength of eleven games in 1952 and six in 1953, he was chosen for the 1953–54 northern hemisphere tour. A flanker, he played in twenty matches including the tests against Ireland and France.

His medical studies took him to Wellington, for whom he also played, and eventually led him to Oxford where he became an expert in renal failure and kidney transplants and set up the renal unit at the Churchill Hospital.

He was a founder member and patron of the British Kidney Patients' Association and among the many patients whose lives he saved was that of John Parsons, the London *Daily Telegraph* tennis writer. 'He was not simply brilliant in his chosen field,' Parsons wrote, 'he offered comfort and reassurance to patients, many of them in despair at their suddenly bleak future.'

Bleakness entered Oliver's own life when his renal unit, and him in particular, were singled out as part of a campaign against the United Kingdom National Health Service's lack of access to dialysis. Campaigners took to newspapers a patient on whom Oliver had discontinued dialysis because the patient had had a stroke, had severe psychological difficulties and could not lead a normal life (even with renal care).

Oliver had to suffer accusations that he was playing God and that he'd sentenced the patient to death. Oliver defended his decision publicly, but thereby breached patient confidentiality. 'It was wrong to keep the poor fellow alive to go through more problems,' Oliver was quoted as saying.

His decision was endorsed by the Oxfordshire District Health Authority, which also rejected suggestions that Oliver practised 'passive euthanasia'.

Labour Members of Parliament led the campaign, largely because they said the National Health Service provided for thirty-three people in a million to have dialysis, whereas it had been twenty-three in a million a decade before. The rate was one of the poorest in Europe; they said that in the United States, nearly ninety places a million were provided.

'The wounds of this attack never really healed,' *The Times* said twelve years later when Oliver died. From being praised for saving perhaps hundreds, he'd been pilloried for not being able to save one.

Oliver cut back on his medical work when the fuss died down and took up woodturning.

ENTER HILDA

The second-last match on France's first tour of New Zealand, in 1961, was a loss to South Canterbury. It's remembered almost as much for grandmother Hilda Madsen storming on to the field and punching Michel Crauste in the back as it is for the upset local win.

For Hilda, it was all a bit too much when Crauste picked up local second-five Ted Smith and dumped him. The crowd roared its approval as Hilda, using a walking stick for mobility rather than as an offensive weapon, entered the arena and went up to Crauste and launched into her one-punch attack from the rear.

Crauste looked around, surprised. Police moved in and took Hilda away and said later it would have been ridiculous to charge her with anything.

French journalist Denis Lalanne put a bit of a gloss on things when he said Crauste had Smith in a headlock and Hilda shouted out, 'You hooligan!'

Hilda recalled: 'I saw red when that Frenchman dragged him [Smith] up like a sack of flour. I hit him hard but I don't think it hurt. I think he got a bit of a shock though. I won't be able to go up the street for a month. I suppose I would do the same thing again, I don't know.'

Hilda, her husband Rex, sons Joe and Pye and nephew Stu Birtles had made the trip from Oamaru for the day.

Ray Vercoe, nineteen, was the youngest player on the ground and recalled years later that he was closest to Crauste at the time of the incident. 'Crauste stiff-armed Ted Smith under the chops and then sat him down again. It happened fairly quickly. She appeared and gave him one but there were two policemen right behind her to escort her off.'

St John officers were there as well to help Madsen away while referee Pat Murphy spoke to the players. What he said wasn't recorded and the French probably wouldn't have understood him anyway. Even if they were of a mind to lend him an ear, which would have been doubtful. One of the reasons for the match being a bit testy, at least from a French perspective, was that Murphy penalised them seventeen times but South Canterbury just three times.

What's been lost in the aftermath, the excitement over both South Canterbury's win and Madsen's cameo, was that the local team played much of the match with fourteen men after first five-eighth Grant Richardson had to go off after just a quarter of an hour. (Replacements were not permitted until 1968.)

UNUSUAL GOAL

People in the 40,000 crowd at Lancaster Park in Christchurch in 1963 saw something in a rugby match that they would never see again: the All Blacks winning a test with a goal from a mark.

The match was the second test on England's first tour of New Zealand (the All Blacks had won the first 21–11) and with five minutes to go, the score was 6-all. Don Clarke, the battleship at fullback for the All Blacks, took a catch around halfway and claimed a mark (marks could be claimed anywhere on the field then).

He took the ball back a few metres, placed it and called his brother Ian — playing in his last test — over to hold it. England players charged too soon so Clarke could take the kick unchallenged. It sailed over the bar and prompted the heading in the *Christchurch Star*: 'Don Clarke saves N.Z.

with The Daddy of all kicks.'

It was the last New Zealand goal from a mark in a test, the rare scoring move being phased out in 1977.

A British journalist, Richard Lacey, wrote in the *Observer* that Don Clarke was the real difference between the two sides. 'This giant figure who has so often pulled out something extra at the vital moment, did just that in the thirty-fifth minute of the second half.' (Lacey reflected the rarity of England players playing in New Zealand at the time by remarking that 'no player has lived . . . until he has played rugby in New Zealand'.)

Clarke had also kicked one in Brisbane in a test against Australia in 1957.

The only other goals from marks scored by New Zealand in tests was one by Mark Nicholls against Great Britain in 1930, also at Lancaster Park, and two by Billy Wallace in New Zealand's first test, in Sydney in 1903.

Ian Clarke, incidentally, also scored a goal from a mark (perhaps the only prop to do so). His was against rather than for New Zealand. He'd been invited to play for the Barbarians in the following northern season in the festival match to end the All Blacks' 1963–64 tour. Brother Don kicked a 25 dropout, Ian caught it and claimed a mark, then proceeded to whack the ball between the posts with a dropkick. It put the Barbarians 3–0 up, but the All Blacks played sparkling exhibition rugby after that to win 36–3.

The last player to kick a goal from a mark in first-class rugby was Kit Fawcett, playing for Waikato against Wairarapa-Bush in 1977.

CULTURAL FULFILMENT

Why Maori took to rugby so early and so enthusiastically, and for a long time played in an exuberant manner not often seen with wholly Pakeha teams, was explained once by a Taranaki man whose versatile career ended as the race relations conciliator, Harry Dansey.

His father and uncle were both rugby players — and Maori — of note and after service in the Second World War, he developed a career as a historian, journalist and cartoonist, mostly in Taranaki and Auckland. He was race relations conciliator, the country's second, from 1975 until 1979.

His views on Maori rugby were published in the programme for the Maori match against South Africa in 1965. 'Maori rugby draws its strength and character from hidden sources,' he wrote. 'It has roots in tradition for, though its flesh and bones are European, its heart and spirit are the authentic expression of the old-time Maori love of strenuous, even violent, competitive physical activity. At its best Maori rugby is an act of deep, fierce, manly joy.'

Dansey said the earliest account he had heard of Maori playing rugby came from an old lady who had lived as a child in the shadow of the old Waihi fort near Hawera. 'On this fort were based some of the units which fought Titokowaru in the wars of the 1860s. She said that men of the Armed Constabulary played football among themselves. Maoris who visited the fort saw how the game was played, played it themselves and joined in impromptu matches with the soldiers.'

The teamwork of rugby, the team taking priority over the needs of the individual, complemented the tight-knit clan system of Maori. 'Up to a certain point,' he wrote, 'and perhaps it should not be over-emphasised . . . rugby provided the outlet for energy once taken up by young men who followed as a vocation the trail of Tumataenga, the God of War.

'So physical fitness and strength, keenness of eye, speed of hand, foot and body movements, co-ordination of thought and muscle, the instant recognition of openings and advantages, the anticipation of an opponent's move were the essence of the business of a warrior. So were the sidestep and the swerve, the duck, the dodge, the dive. And so were the clutch, the catch, the clash of man against man.'

Rugby fulfilled a cultural need in the physical sense which had been present ever since the European civilisation 'had struck — for good or ill — at the roots of Maori society'.

REALLY, REF?

The genial Irish referee, Kevin Kelleher, who was in charge of twenty-three internationals between 1960 and 1972, sent only one player from the field — 'And it had to be me,' Colin Meads used to lament. The dismissal, the second of an All Black, happened in the last couple of minutes of the test against Scotland at Murrayfield in December 1967.

Kelleher had earlier cautioned Meads so he saw he had no option when Meads, moving from a disintegrating ruck, had a kick at the ball that was about to be picked up by the Scotland halfback, David Chisholm.

Kelleher didn't hesitate; he blew his whistle and told Meads he had to go. 'You really mean it, ref?' Meads asked. Yes, he really meant it and Meads began the longest, loneliest trudge of his rugby life.

It says something of the calibre of both men, Kelleher and Meads, that the sending off brought them closer together. Kelleher a few years later gave Meads the whistle he had used at Murrayfield, the pair visited each other at their homes on a couple of occasions and they exchanged Christmas cards every year until they died within a year of each other. 'Oh, he wasn't a bad joker,' Meads used to say.

No one seriously thought Meads set out to kick or maim Chisholm, probably not even that small section of the Murrayfield crowd who, according to Norman Mair, the rugby journalist for the *Scotsman*, 'deprived nowadays of public hangings, bayed in triumph'.

Mair, who had played for Scotland, said Meads' action was undeniably dangerous play 'but also I think — and Chisholm thought so, too — one of those innumerable incidents in rugby, which look somewhat worse than they are and very much worse than they feel'.

Mair at different times described Meads as the personification of New Zealand forward play and 'physically and technically, if not temperamentally, the most complete forward I have ever seen'.

The All Blacks went on to Wales after the Scottish test for their last three matches, but Meads was not allowed to play in two of them. An International Rugby Board committee that included All Blacks manager Charlie Saxton suspended Meads for two matches. Saxton, needless to say, dissented. Saxton later told the NZRFU: 'Unfortunately, I was on my own and eventually had to compromise for a penalty of a suspension for the next two games.' Meads was not even given a chance to speak to the committee, although it allowed Kelleher to do so. This incensed New Zealand officials — both in Britain and New Zealand — and one of the NZRFU delegates to the IRB, Ces Blazey, ensured a law change the following year, making provision for accused players to be given a hearing.

A blast from this sent Colin Meads to the dressing room.

A PRIDE OF LIONS

When the 1966 Lions arrived in Wellington, a doctor in his seventies paid them a visit, bearing a gift. He was Martin Tweed, and he had with him a photograph of an earlier Lions team of which he had been a member.

If some of the Lions had not heard of the team, it would have been no surprise. It was a team comprising English and Scottish players, known at the time as 'the English team' and which toured Argentina in 1910, and has since been adopted as one of the series of British and Irish Lions sides. Tweed, who had been studying at Guy's Hospital, was twenty at the time and played at both centre and in the forwards. They had one match against Argentina, which did not count as a test from a British point of view but has since become the first test by an Argentine side.

129

'It was a wonderful tour, a marvellous experience,' Tweed said in 1966. 'The rugby wasn't bad in the Argentine though probably not of a first-class standard.'

Thanks to the retrospective capturing of various teams by the British and Irish Lions organisation, Tweed became one of a handful of New Zealanders to play for the Lions — and probably the least known.

A teammate on that tour was another New Zealand medical student, Alex Palmer, who had also played on the wing for England.

(Tweed gained a later fame in 1943 when a former prime minister, Gordon Coates, collapsed and died in his office in Parliament. Tweed was one of two doctors called in to try to save him.)

Two earlier New Zealand Lions were Pat McEvedy and Arthur O'Brien with the British team in New Zealand in 1904, and McEvedy again with the Anglo-Welsh in 1908. McEvedy was later a president of the New Zealand union.

Another New Zealander, Jules Malfroy, a lawyer, was also in an unofficial Lions team that toured Argentina in 1927 and has since joined the British and Irish list.

With an increasing number of New Zealanders playing in Britain after the game went professional, it was inevitable more would become Lions. Among the recent crop have been Riki Flutey, Sean Maitland, Jared Payne, Ben Te'o and Mako Vunipola. Flutey is the only one to have played both against (for Wellington in 2005) and for the Lions.

Of course, the Lions — the pride of British and Irish rugby and the ultimate accolade for a player there — have also been coached by two New Zealanders, Graham Henry and Warren Gatland.

CENTENARY MARKED

Through a mixture of enthusiasm, skill and some hard work, a man not known as a rugby author produced in 1970 a book described as the most fitting acknowledgement of the game's known history in New Zealand of a hundred years.

The author was Gordon Slatter, forty-eight, a schoolteacher from

Christchurch, and his book was *On the Ball*, subtitled a centennial history of New Zealand rugby. Brian O'Brien, the editor of the monthly *Sports Digest* magazine and himself a font of rugby knowledge, marvelled at Slatter's industry and wondered how on earth the title had not been used before in a country that gave birth to it.

'Slatter's monumental, informative and entertaining work is nearly four hundred large pages of the most readable rugby history of them all,' O'Brien enthused.

Slatter began his history, as he should, with the game in Nelson in 1870, but he thereafter wended his way through a hundred years of rugby with some chapters on aspects not often written about, at least not in books. And for each chapter, he chose to begin with a signal game — 2nd NZEF v Wales in 1946 began the Services Rugby chapter; Otago Boys' High School v Christchurch Boys' High School in 1963 began the chapter on Secondary School Rugby, and so on.

There were chapters about each of the main test-playing countries with, again, one particular match being featured. Slatter was not predictable. For Wales, for example, he wrote about the 1935 test in Cardiff rather than 1905.

Slatter was not a rugby 'name'. If he was known at all beyond the circles in which he moved, it was through other books such as *A Gun in My Hand* (a story about a soldier readjusting to civilian life) or *The Pagan Game*, a novel about college football.

O'Brien described him as 'the man on the bank, the man who has made New Zealand rugby what it is, who has embraced and been its backbone . . . it seems to us fitting that a member of the ordinary paying public should contribute this history'.

Slatter taught at several schools but was mostly associated with Christchurch Boys' High, where he was the history master and First XV coach.

When he died in 2002, a victim of a car crash, one colleague said of him: 'He was a great yarner. I used to love just sitting around and talking to him. He was a truly lovely man.'

KING JOHN

Whether you date the Lions from 1930, as most sensible people do, or from 1888, as the British and Irish Lions organisation itself does, there surely could be no argument about which has been the best Lions team in New Zealand. The 1971 team is the only one that has won a series against the All Blacks.

They were a team of all the talents, and quite possibly the best of all time, shading the team that went to South Africa in 1974. The 1971 Lions had forwards such as Willie John McBride, Mervyn Davies, John Pullin and Ian McLauchlan, among many others, and backs whose names signpost greatness in rugby: Gareth Edwards, Barry John, Mike Gibson, Gerald Davies, J.P.R. Williams. The man most responsible for the success was the coach, Carwyn James. He had a quiet, personal charm and an understated intelligence that made people warm to him.

If New Zealanders had to name one 1971 Lion who made a difference,

Barry John runs in defence in the first test at Carisbrook. Other players are John Bevan, Tane Norton, Colin Meads, John Pullin, Alan McNaughton and J.P.R. Williams.

they'd probably name Barry John, that most brilliant of first five-eighths who seemed to be able to win games on his own. But for James, John would not have been in New Zealand in 1971.

John suffered a broken nose against France in the 1971 Five Nations and took a while to recover. He felt fed up with rugby. He received his letter 'inviting' him to tour with the Lions and didn't bother to reply. James went calling to find out why. John told him he wouldn't be going; he wanted a break from rugby and certainly didn't want to spend three months of the British summer playing the game.

Perhaps only James could have persuaded John otherwise. They both came from the tiny west Wales village of Cefneithin in the Carmarthen coalfields about 15 km north of Llanelli; perhaps it was that link, forged by birth, that made the difference. James offered John concessions — come to New Zealand on your own terms, he told him. Play when you want. The astute James knew John would never agree to being treated as 'special' and knew he'd eventually get his man. Ten days before the team was due to assemble, John phoned James and agreed. John did become a bit of a special case on tour, being excused training when he felt the need for a rest, but none of the players appeared to resent it.

'He played rugby on a different plane from anyone else I ever saw,' Mervyn Davies once said. 'He was on a different, superior wavelength.'

ROUGH JUSTICE

The peremptory sending home of Keith Murdoch from a northern hemisphere tour in 1972 stands as an indelible stain on rugby's history.

There was fault in Murdoch's action in hitting a Welsh security guard when he was seemingly provoked on the night of the Welsh test, but there was fault too with the way the incident was handled. Murdoch had no opportunity to state his case, as a player would today, and the decision to send him home was arrived at in a telephone call between John Tallent, the ultimate British official, and Jack Sullivan, the chairman of the NZRFU. In short, Tallent told Sullivan that if Murdoch was not sent home, the rest of the tour would be in jeopardy; and in any case, a replacement for manager Ernie Todd would be sought.

The problem for Sullivan was this: abandon the tour (even though the NZRFU was not benefiting financially from it) or go through the humiliation of having a manager publicly disgraced. Far easier for Sullivan to sacrifice Murdoch, a player with a complex combination of immense strength, gentle demeanour but capable of sudden violence.

So Murdoch left after thirteen games of a 32-match tour. His day went from towering triumph when he scored New Zealand's only try against Wales, the test that mattered most, to one of anger, sorrow and eternal silence.

Murdoch left his flight home in Singapore, went to Perth, and thereafter, as far as the public was concerned, spent most of the rest of his life working in remote parts of Australia. He made occasional trips home to see family and friends, and he had sustained work on a couple of occasions in New Zealand,

Getty

Keith Murdoch on his way, flanked by a British official, Stanley Couchman, right, and reporters.

134

but the public seldom knew where he was.

He steadfastly refused to speak to the occasional reporter who ran him down, but that was not unusual; he hadn't spoken much to reporters in the previous eight years of his rugby life either, including being an All Black in South Africa in 1970 where he made his test debut.

Murdoch was the only player sent home from a tour by the All Blacks; other players got themselves into trouble, some even spending time in jail, others making court appearances, but none suffered the ultimate penalty that was inflicted upon Murdoch.

When Murdoch died of renal failure in north-west Western Australia in 2018, along with the usual sadness that greets the death of anyone was a regret that the final chapter in the tale could never be written. Murdoch's side of events, never expressed over forty-six years, now never could be.

A TOUR CANCELLED

The men who ran New Zealand rugby walked solemnly into the room where they made their decisions, big and small. It was Wednesday, 11 April 1973. The decision they were about to make was one of the biggest in the 81-year administrative history of the game.

There were old All Blacks captains among them, men whose passion for the game had been tested on the field; now it was being tested again. There was Charlie Saxton, one of the most liked men in rugby. Ben Couch, a Maori politician whose race stopped him from touring South Africa as a player twenty-four years before. There was Frank Kilby, a captain of the thirties and a manager of the sixties. Ces Blazey, for whom the word punctilious might have been invented. And there was Jack Sullivan, the All Black who became the NZRFU chairman, the oil company driver who became its managing director. There were others.

The question they were confronted with in Wellington that day was both simple and complex. They had earlier agreed to a tour by a South African rugby team. No details had been made public, but those in the know thought it would be a tour of twenty-five matches with four test matches.

Confirmation of the tour was on the table. Also there was a letter from the Prime Minister, Norman Kirk, that the union had received five days before. The issue was whether New Zealand should host a tour by a whites-only team from racially divided South Africa. It had been a contentious issue for years and Kirk, who had been elected the year before, had said previously he would not interfere.

But he changed his mind, he said, because of the possibility of widespread civil disruption and because a state of civil emergency may be needed. Kirk told the union in a letter that he 'was regretfully compelled to require the Rugby Union to inform the South African Rugby Board that its invitation must be deferred. I would have preferred and have indeed worked hard to avoid the need for such a direction.'

The rugby men, faced with a direction, a demand, from the lawful leader of the country, knew they had no choice, though some argued for conditions such as compensation. Shortly after three hours' deliberation, Sullivan read a statement that had been prepared by Kilby, the acting secretary.

The words dripped with disappointment: 'With deep regret the Council [of the NZRFU] are of the opinion that although they do not accept or agree with many of the statements in the Prime Minister's letter, they have no alternative but to accede, under protest, to this direction . . .'

CAPTAIN ANDY

When Andy Leslie led his beloved Petone club on a novel and controversial tour of South Africa towards the end of summer in 1974, he thought it a nice way to end his career. He was twenty-nine, he'd played more than a hundred games for Wellington. Playing for New Zealand, he was convinced, had passed him by. Enough was enough. Time to go.

He even wrote to his wife Lesley from South Africa and said he wouldn't go away again without her. But it was just the start of a whole new career — as captain of the All Blacks. Barely a month after returning from South Africa, Leslie was named to play for New Zealand for the first time, and he was made captain.

Two trials were played at Athletic Park in Wellington on 17 April 1974 for coach J.J. Stewart, in his second year, to find the players to take on a tour of Australia. Alex Wyllie and Alan Sutherland were the number eights in the first match, and Leslie and Greg McGee in the second. Leslie captained the trial team.

In the way of things in those days, the players all crammed into the function room at Athletic Park afterwards for the naming

Andy Leslie

of the team. The chairman of the New Zealand union, Jack Sullivan, read the names in position order by the old method of initials, surname and province. When he got to the number eights, he began 'A.R. . . .' Andy Leslie, whose given names were Andrew Roy, immediately thought he was finished because Sutherland from the first trial was also 'A.R.' (for Alan Richard). But no. It was Leslie's name that Sullivan read. Leslie was stunned. Even more stunning was that he was named captain, even though the previous leader, Ian Kirkpatrick, was also in the side.

Leslie led Stewart's new All Blacks to Australia and Fiji in 1974, then to Ireland at the end of the year for the Irish union's centenary. He was captain again the next year against Scotland in the soaking conditions at Eden Park, then rounded off his 'second' career by leading the team through the South African tour of 1976.

Leslie, who'd been in partnership in a menswear business in Petone with the great fullback of the 1940s and 50s, Bob Scott, later coached Wellington and had a stint in Ireland. He also served a term as president of the New Zealand union. Leslie was part of an unusual sporting dynasty. His father, also Andy, had played soccer for Hibernian in Edinburgh and also for New Zealand. 'Young' Andy's two sons, John and Martin, played provincial and Super rugby in New Zealand and both became 'kilted Kiwis', playing tests for Scotland.

LAKE EDEN

It was a match that probably shouldn't have been played. Rugby prides itself for carrying on in all weather, but this was both dangerous and ridiculous. It was 1975 and the All Blacks' only test of the year, against Scotland.

It started to rain in Auckland on the Friday when both teams had finished training. It rained all afternoon. It rained all night. It was still raining on the morning of the match. The Scottish manager, George Burrell, and the New Zealand union chairman, Jack Sullivan, met at Eden Park hours before kick-off. They saw that parts of the ground were under water; they saw that gutters on the main stand roof had given way; they saw that duckboards had been laid to ease spectators' passage.

A harness racing meeting at nearby Alexandra Park was called off because conditions were deemed to be too unsafe for both man and beast. Not so at the rugby. The game would go on.

The Scots felt especially cursed by the weather. They knew, or at least experienced players such as captain Ian McLauchlan and prop Sandy Carmichael knew, that if they were to have any chance of beating the All Blacks, everything would need to be in their favour. The rain ended that chance. It wasn't that the big wet necessarily favoured the All Blacks, just that it increased the possibility of mistakes.

The All Blacks, who'd played in similar conditions in Sydney the year before, adapted well. The Scots didn't adapt at all. Their celebrated wing-fullback, Andy Irvine, could hardly catch a ball all day; if there was any luck, it was with the All Blacks. Balls bounced and slid for the All Blacks; they plopped down and sat still for the Scots.

Nothing should detract from the All Blacks' performance. It was masterly. Four tries to none — two by the incomparable Bryan Williams and one each by Hamish Macdonald and Duncan Robertson. Joe Karam, playing his only test in New Zealand, converted them all, kicking four from four with a soaked leather ball off a wet, muddy ground.

Everything seemed to go right for the All Blacks; very little for the Scots. Irvine had been put on the wing because of the commanding tour form by Bruce Hay, who was at fullback, playing the first of his twenty-six matches. He and Grant Batty went for a high ball and Hay came down with a broken arm. He tried to play on but couldn't.

It was a day to forget for the Scots.

All Blacks, clad in white for the first time since 1930, and Scots take to 'Lake Eden'.

BROTHERS BLAZEY

Three brothers called Blazey had a profound influence on New Zealand sport, particularly rugby, for much of the twentieth century (and even beyond).

Bill and Emily Blazey had four children — Dick in 1896, Grace in 1898, Henry (Harry) in 1904 and Cecil (Ces) in 1909. Dick took up refereeing when he finished playing and was a leading Canterbury official until his death. Harry's main activities were also in Canterbury, though he served a term as NZRFU president. Harry was also a member of the organising committee of the 1974 Commonwealth Games.

The youngest brother, Ces, was the best known. He was a colonel in the Army Service Corps in the Pacific during the war and entered rugby administration through his work for university rugby. He became a senior insurance company executive at the same time as he rose through rugby's administrative ranks in Wellington, where he came to be regarded internationally as an expert on rugby law and, just a little less so, on rugby lore. (He rose similarly in the administration of athletics.)

He took over as chairman of the NZRFU from Jack Sullivan in 1976 and was the top man for the next decade; his retirement was coincidental to the 1985–86 South African controversy, but not because of it. Blazey always maintained he represented the council of the NZRFU and therefore expressed its collective view and not his own; nevertheless, there's reason to believe he personally did not want the All Blacks to go to South Africa in 1985 (and they didn't, as it turned out).

It was the South African issue that forced Blazey out of athletics. He'd been chairman of the New Zealand Amateur Athletics Association but stood down voluntarily in 1981 because of his association with the South African tour of that year.

Blazey was justifiably regarded as an honest man true to principles (which angered some politicians who didn't understand such things). Even in retirement in the Karori home where he'd lived all his married life, some rugby administrators continued to seek him out for his institutional knowledge, which was vast, or his advice, which was invariably sound.

He was equally highly regarded among members of the International Rugby Board who regularly sent him suggestions for rugby law changes, or drafts of proposed changes, seeking his advice. Blazey wrote an unpublished autobiography which was more a chronological account of his rugby travelling and is replete with accounts of meetings with those who controlled the destiny of the game.

MCKECHNIE'S MOMENT

It's a story often told. How Wales led the All Blacks 12–10 in 1978 with just a couple of minutes to go; how Wales were penalised at a defensive lineout and how replacement Brian McKechnie kicked the goal that won the test.

And oh yes, how Andy Haden fell theatrically out of the lineout in a vain bid to win a penalty. The other All Blacks lock, Frank Oliver, also had a lean on but nothing to rival Haden's.

It remains a scarred memory in Wales, how the Welsh say they were cheated out of victory against New Zealand and how the referee, Roger Quittenton, had been conned. It's also one of those match incidents, like the disputed New Zealand try in Cardiff in 1905, that's embellished in the retelling and imagination takes the place of reality.

Was Quittenton conned? He said after the game and forever more that he penalised the Welsh lock, Geoff Wheel, for interfering with Oliver when the ball was thrown in by Bobby Windsor. He said he did not see Haden's lurch to the left, but even if he had, he wouldn't have penalised him because it had no material effect on the game.

McKechnie, thrust under the searchlight of scrutiny, hadn't seen Haden's antics either. It was only later when he saw a BBC recording that he realised what the growing fuss was about.

McKechnie had not even expected to be on the tour. He was not picked

Brian McKechnie

in the original tour party and only added when fullback Bevan Wilson had to pull out because of injury. McKechnie had been a reserve against Ireland in the previous test but was not wanted in the reserves for Wales. On the night before the game, he had a few beers in the house bar of the All Blacks' home away from home, the Seabank Hotel in Porthcawl. Captain Graham Mourie wandered in and had a quiet word, saying he might be needed on the morrow.

The next morning, coach Jack Gleeson popped his head into McKechnie's room and said, 'You'd better get your gear ready Colt, you're in the reserves.' McKechnie had the call-up because halfback Mark Donaldson had been injured at training and replaced by Dave Loveridge. There was no other halfback so the expectation was that if anything happened to Loveridge, Doug Bruce would take over and McKechnie would cover first five-eighth. But fullback Clive Currie was injured early in the game and McKechnie got on the field.

He was also the man in a crisis when he was the facing batsman to Trevor Chappell's underarm delivery in the one-day match against Australia in Melbourne in 1981.

HOW GRAND THE SLAM

New Zealand first achieved the grand slam — victory over each of England, Ireland, Scotland and Wales on the one tour — in 1978, but they'd gone close before that, and even pursued the elusive prize before it had a name.

South Africa achieved the grand slam on four occasions, all of them before

New Zealand did it, and it was something of an unfilled column in tour records for the All Blacks.

New Zealand's first chance was in 1905 but of course the 3–0 loss to Wales put a stop to that. The next opportunity was in 1924 and the All Blacks won all their twenty-eight games in the United Kingdom and Ireland, but they couldn't number the Scots among their opponents. The Scottish union refused to have anything to do with the All Blacks, partly because of the Scots' resentment at England organising the tour on their own, and partly because of residual concerns that the All Blacks in 1905 were paid.

Tours came and went and still the slam couldn't be captured: losses to Wales in 1935 and 1953, then a draw against Scotland in 1963. The next tour, in 1967, seemed to be New Zealand's time, such was the quality of the side, but again the slam was denied them, this time because they couldn't play Ireland due to an outbreak of foot-and-mouth disease in England. The next team, in 1972–73, was much criticised but even so only a draw with Ireland prevented them from beating all four.

So it came to 1978, when the side led by Graham Mourie and coached by Jack Gleeson famously lost to Munster, New Zealand's first loss to any Irish team, but won the four tests, three of them, against Ireland, Wales and Scotland, won only narrowly in the dying minutes, but won they were.

The phrase 'grand slam' comes from bridge and has been applied to other sports to signify victory in all possible contests. It appears to have been first used in a rugby sense — used in print anyway — on 25 February 1957 when the English tabloid, *Daily Mirror*, ran a headline on a story about England beating France and with just Scotland to come: 'England bid for the grand slam'.

Others soon picked up on it. Uel Titley, the rugby writer for *The Times*, previewed the Scottish match on 16 March 1957 and said: 'The last time when England achieved the grand slam . . . was as long ago as the 1927–28 season.' The *Daily Telegraph* on the Monday, after England had won, had the phrase in a headline: 'Handsome victory earns England grand slam'. After that initial breakthrough, New Zealand achieved it also in 2005, 2008 and 2010.

'FOR JACK'

The All Blacks beat Midlands 33–7 at the Welford Road ground in Leicester in 1979. Just another New Zealand win. Just another tour match. There was no 'just' about it.

This was a game the All Blacks wanted not only to win but to win by playing well and enjoying themselves. They wanted it to be a good win 'for Jack'. And it was.

Jack Gleeson had been the coach when the New Zealand team first achieved the grand slam the previous year, his fourth year in a broken sequence of coaching the national team. It was also his last.

Gleeson first coached the All Blacks on an internal tour in 1972 when he was manager of the team as well. No doctor, no physiotherapist, no assistant and certainly none of the other outriders of the modern game.

By then, it had already been decided that Bob Duff would coach the team on the northern tour of 1972–73. The NZRFU had a haphazard succession plan at the time, not helped by unavailabilities, and J.J. Stewart was coach in 1974–76. Gleeson took a second national team to Argentina late in 1976 when no official tests were played, then had the top job against the Lions in 1977, in Italy and France later in the year, then against Australia and in the United Kingdom and Ireland in 1978.

He knew he was unwell towards the end of the grand slam tour but kept it to only a few confidants. Sipping sparingly at some white concoction that looked suspiciously like milk, he acknowledged he'd had a bit of back trouble and would have it seen to when he got home.

Early in 1979, he knew he had terminal cancer and players drove and flew from all over New Zealand to see him in his Feilding home.

Eric Watson meanwhile took over as coach and he had the team in England and Scotland at the start of the British season when, in Leicester on the night before the game against Midlands, word came through that Gleeson had died.

It was a sad Saturday. The manager, Russ Thomas, rang Gleeson's widow Ida and she wished 'the boys' all the best. Captain Graham Mourie, who had been with Gleeson in Argentina and France as well as the grand slam tour, spoke for the players. 'To me, Jack epitomised what rugby is about. His approach to life, his approach to the game. His is a great loss to New Zealand. We went out to play the kind of rugby Jack wanted, to play well and to make it enjoyable.'

THE RISE OF SEVENS

Seven-a-side rugby was the game that used to be played early in the season when a full line-up of fifteen may not have been available, or as a fundraising day for various noble causes. For most of rugby's life, sevens was just a bit of fun.

But then the International Rugby Board, never previously all that keen, discovered there was money to be made and it began a world circuit which eventually saw readmission to the Olympic Games and series for men and women.

Sevens began as a fundraising gesture at Melrose in the Scottish Borders. A local butcher, Ned Haig, suggested in 1883 an afternoon of seven-a-side rugby to raise funds for the club; the initial idea had been to invite other Borders clubs for a rugby tournament, but full matches would have taken too much time. Hence Haig's brainwave.

Six years later, it seemed, the first sevens matches were played in New Zealand. The Otago union chose to run a post-season tournament in late September 1889 at Carisbrook to raise money for Dunedin Hospital. All the Dunedin senior clubs, plus a couple of junior ones, entered. Games were of fifteen minutes' duration and the usual laws of the game applied.

One of the local papers commented that some of the canny clubs, especially Dunedin which won the final, picked only the slim and the swift; the beefy forwards were deemed not suitable for such a fast-paced game in which speed and passing took precedence over grunting in scrums and mauls.

The idea caught on because seven-a-side tournaments became commonplace throughout New Zealand thereafter, but they always ranked well behind the main game for importance and significance.

When the Hong Kong Rugby Union in the 1970s decided a sevens tournament was a popular, money-making attraction, some New Zealand provincial teams took part until Hong Kong said it wanted a national team or nothing. New Zealand bowed to the inevitable and sent a formal team for the first time in 1983, losing to Western Samoa in a quarterfinal. New Zealand's only previous sevens team had been for a commemorative tournament in Scotland in 1973, played as part of the Scottish union's centenary. The first success in Hong Kong was in 1986 when New Zealand beat the French Barbarians in the final.

It was only with the prospect of the Olympics that the International Rugby Board slowly took an official interest in the game and began its World Cup for sevens and the world circuit.

THE COCK O' THE NORTH

A missed conversion in the last minute spared the All Blacks even more blushes one day in 1979 when they were embarrassed enough by England's Northern Division 21–9. The twelve-point loss equalled the margin of the losses to Munster the year before and to the Barbarians in Cardiff in 1973. Had the conversion made the final score 23–9, it would have been the heaviest defeat suffered by New Zealand in the northern hemisphere at that time — beating by a point the 13–0 tally by England in 1936.

Record or not, Graham Mourie's All Blacks were well beaten at the tiny ground of Cross Green in Otley, about 15 km from Leeds. The ground officially held about 5000, but it was estimated about 7000 crammed in and small boys climbed trees overlooking the ground, hanging on for dear life in the stiff wind that threatened to blow them to the Yorkshire Dales.

The North were led by the redoubtable Bill Beaumont and there were internationals aplenty with him. One of them, prop Colin White, was a forestry worker and nicknamed 'The Claw'. That was because he had three fingers on one hand, having cut two of them off with a chainsaw. He got in his Land Rover and drove to hospital, but halfway there remembered his fingers so he went back to fetch them. But by the time he got to a hospital, it was too late to reattach the fingers. They were tough men. They were also experienced men. They had five who had captained England, seven who had or would be Lions.

The North scored four tries to New Zealand's one and even with the wind, there was a sense the All Blacks could never win this match. The North defended through their forwards and attacked mainly through their tactically minded halfback, Steve Smith, and their goal-kicking first five-eighth, Alan Old.

Seven of the North played for England the following week in the test at Twickenham when the All Blacks got home by a single point. Crucially for New Zealand, the England selectors chose not to take Old and went instead for Les Cusworth.

Fran Cotton, the lantern-jawed prop, especially liked the game. It was his fourth victory over New Zealand: North-West Counties 1972, England (in Auckland) in 1973 and the second test for the Lions in 1977. Cotton was ready for any funny stuff too. Coach Des Seabrook said he'd been worried that Andy Haden might interfere with Beaumont. 'If he touches him, I'll knock his head off,' Cotton growled.

For the record, New Zealand's heaviest loss to an England team was 21–38 at Twickenham in 2012.

CENTENARY TEST

At times there's been enmity between the two great rugby nations, New Zealand and Wales, and at times there's been deep friendship. On the field, they've been the greatest of rivals. Off the field, Welsh fans yearn for the day their team again takes down the All Blacks — and few would not know that hasn't happened since 1953.

There's always been deep respect. Respect from one rugby country to another; two countries which put rugby ahead of other sports.

Captain Graham Mourie scores in the centenary test. The Welsh halfback is Terry Holmes and the touch judge, David Burnett of Ireland.

It was a mark of that respect that New Zealand were invited to share the Welsh union's centenary in 1980. For all that, though, Wales loaded the dice. Not only would there be a centenary test as a climax, the All Blacks would also have a game against each of the clubs that had previously beaten them: Cardiff, Llanelli, Swansea and Newport.

It was a short tour that gave much: the decision to send off Graeme Higginson in the Llanelli match that was reversed because of entreaties from both teams to referee Alan Hosie; the bridge-building and fence-mending that went on behind the scenes, especially an unpublicised visit by John Ashworth to Bridgend; the general air of Wales really keeping a welcome in the hillsides for their visitors from far away.

The test match was won by New Zealand in a manner befitting such an occasion and belied some patchy form by the All Blacks earlier in the year. It was the crowning match in the brief New Zealand coaching career of Eric

Watson, it was a game close to excellence for every All Black who played in it. They knew it was a special performance for a special occasion.

The captain, Graham Mourie, had two more years as an All Black, but perhaps the centenary test was his finest. It was appropriate that he scored one of the All Blacks' four tries, a dive in the corner that ended a move that had begun when the Welsh centre, Dai Richards, grabbed an intercept and hared toward the goal-line; but the peerless Bruce Robertson counter-attacked and Mourie was in the right place, as he mostly was, to finish off.

That night at the test dinner, the president of the Welsh union, Cliff Jones — who had played in the winning Welsh side against the All Blacks in 1935 — stood and proclaimed: 'I can go to my maker happy because today I have seen the greatest display of back row play by Graham Mourie.'

THE TOUR

Rugby has known no more rancorous tour, none that split a nation so much. Phrases such as '1981' and 'the Springbok tour' years later conjured up searing images: of barbed wire, of grim police lines, of street fighting, and occasionally some rugby.

The South Africans played fourteen matches in New Zealand in 1981, from the first in Gisborne to the last in Auckland. Protests about playing host to a rugby team from apartheid South Africa became as violent as police had predicted. One match, the second, against Waikato, was called off when protesters invaded the ground and wouldn't move. Another, against South Canterbury in Timaru, was called off partly because the ground was difficult to protect and partly to give police a break.

At one point, police and rugby officials met and discussed whether the tour should be called off. The government didn't want the tour but did little to stop it and certainly didn't tell the NZRFU to withdraw the invitation, as Norman Kirk had told it eight years earlier.

South Africans had toured before amid protests, in the United Kingdom

Ron Palenski Collection

*Prop Gary Knight on the ground in the third test — he'd been hit by a flour 'bomb'
dropped from an aircraft flown by a protester.*

in 1969–70 and in Australia in 1971, but nothing of the scale encountered in New Zealand in 1981. That was partly because New Zealand was smaller but also because rugby means more in New Zealand than it does in the UK or Australia. Passions were always going to be more inflamed in New Zealand.

It was a tour that polarised. People were either for it or against it. It divided families; it divided rugby itself.

Games were played behind coils of barbed wire with police facing the crowd; jumbo bins and other heavy objects were in strategic positions around grounds to keep protesters at bay. Protesters time and again clashed with lines of police wielding batons.

Some protests were peaceful: a motorway sit-down in Wellington, a vigil at Parliament. Some were violent, especially in Wellington and Auckland.

Thousands of protesters took to the streets on match days. But thousands of people also went to the matches, implicitly welcoming the visitors half the country detested. Published crowd figures showed that 360,500 people were at matches; it's doubtful if that number actively protested.

The vast majority of New Zealanders would have had a view on the tour but neither protested nor watched games.

Whatever the value of the rugby, the tour was the reason for the worst rioting in New Zealand; worse than 1932 Depression riots, worse than a labour dispute in Waihi in 1912, worse than waterfront riots in 1913, all events previously held as being bellwethers for widespread public disorder.

ABSENT CAPTAIN

When the South African rugby team played Taranaki in 1981, the third game of that blighted tour, the man who could have been captaining the local team was spreading fertiliser on his dairy farm.

No previous absence of a player from the playing field, and none since, could have attracted so much public attention. The absentee was, of course, Graham Mourie, the Taranaki and New Zealand captain who had declared that he could not, in all conscience, play a team from South Africa as long as that country's apartheid policy continued.

Mourie's public announcement over the summer of 1980–81, once it became clear the tour was going ahead, shocked some and delighted others. As on all things South Africa, the country was divided. Mourie had discussed the South African tour with several people during the preceding centenary tour of Wales at the end of 1980. He made his decision he would not play but held back on making it public so as not to detract from the Welsh tour.

Mourie noted in his diary: 'I believe the tour is wrong — for morality, for rugby because the controversy and the effects of the tour will be bad for the game. While it might be said I have fuelled the controversy, I resent that I should have to make the choice . . .'

He was met with understanding by some rugby officials, especially chairman Ces Blazey and Russ Thomas, who had been manager on two of Mourie's tours. But Ron Don, an implacable advocate of South Africa who had managed Mourie's first two tours, saw him as 'a misinformed, misguided youngster'.

Mourie was asked to join in various protests but declined them all, saying his absence from the Taranaki match and the three tests was his protest. He also turned down a disingenuous offer to go to South Africa 'to see for himself'.

Mourie was joined in his opposition to the tour by other All Blacks with whom he'd toured, Bruce Robertson, Gary Seear and Mervyn Jaffray.

Mourie had begun the international season by captaining the All Blacks in a series against Scotland and during the South African matches was pragmatic enough to note the play of replacement flankers and wonder whether they would be good enough to keep their places and therefore force him out. He need not have worried because by the end of the year, when the All Blacks went to Romania — a country at the time with a regime as repressive as South Africa's — and France, he was restored as captain.

TRAPPER'S TEST

The Lions of 1983, the team managed by Willie John McBride, coached by Jim Telfer — both of them former Lions of renown — and captained by an Irish army officer, Ciaran Fitzgerald, lost its four tests, lost also to Auckland and Canterbury and left, according to those usually understanding judges, Rod Chester and Neville McMillan, little to remember.

But as so often is the case, it could all have been different. They lost the first test in Christchurch 16–12, the All Blacks securing the win only in the last minute with an Allan Hewson dropped goal. And the next test, in Wellington a fortnight later, is remembered as 'Trapper's test'. The All Blacks' halfback, Dave Loveridge, more than any other single player, controlled the fortunes of this match in a manner seldom seen.

Wellington turned on its worst weather. The night before the game, snow fell in central Wellington. The next day, the snow and the rain had gone to higher ground, but a bitterly cold southerly remained, one of those winds that roared in off Cook Strait with Athletic Park in its direct path.

On such days, there used to be two questions, one before the game and one at halftime. Before the game, the question was, 'Take the wind?' Invariably, the answer was yes. And at halftime, having taken the wind, the question became, 'Enough points?'

On this occasion, Andy Dalton won the toss and told referee Francis Palmade that New Zealand would take the wind. As expected, the rugby was not flamboyant. No risks were to be taken. With nearly twenty minutes up, the All Blacks won ruck ball about ten metres out from the Lions' line. Loveridge ran on the blindside, sold a dummy and with the ball tucked under his right arm, got over for the try. Hewson converted and added a penalty goal ten minutes later.

That was the end of the scoring. Were nine points enough to hold the Lions out?

Dave Loveridge ... 'among the greatest half-backs of all time'.

No, would have been the reply, especially not with one of the best kickers in the game, Ollie Campbell, in the Lions team and a gale at his back. But the speculators had not reckoned on Loveridge taking control.

The New Zealand forwards clung to the ball, released it sparingly and only when told by Loveridge. He then decided what would happen next. Every decision was the right one, every run back into the forwards to set up another ruck, every deft kick, every pass to Wayne Smith. The All Blacks pack was magnificent — Loveridge was beyond even that. As Chester was left to conclude, 'it ranked him among the greatest halfbacks of all time'.

END OF AN ERA

Rugby's embrace of South Africa during the apartheid era came to a painful and lingering end in the mid-1980s.

New Zealand had been scheduled to tour South Africa in 1985 and while there was more opposition within rugby than previously, the national union still decided to press ahead. The Prime Minister, David Lange, tried and failed to convince the union to do otherwise.

The tour was stopped because of legal action by two men, Patrick Finnigan and Philip Recordon, who were plaintiffs in an action against the union that challenged the tour decision on the grounds that the tour would infringe rule 2a of the union: 'The objects of the Union shall be: (a) to control, promote, foster and develop the game of amateur Rugby Union Football throughout New Zealand.'

After a legal dispute about whether the pair had 'standing' to bring such a suit, a High Court judge, Maurice (later Sir Maurice) Casey, allowed Finnigan and Recordon an injunction that had the effect of stopping the tour while the legal case continued. But the union, seeing the writing plainly on the wall, said it was running out of time and abandoned the tour. The All Blacks went to Argentina instead.

But the players were determined to have their South African tour and they went ahead, with assistance from authorities in South Africa, the following year as 'the Cavaliers'. It led to one of the most divisive periods of New Zealand rugby. Those who went to South Africa were banned for one game (because the NZRFU had no power to do anything more) and declared ineligible for another (because they had not been resident for the requisite number of days). Consequently, a 'new' All Blacks team beat France in one match and lost to Australia in another. When the two groups of All Blacks came together for the remaining two tests against the Wallabies, there was talk of dissent and disagreement within the team. To no one's surprise, they lost the Bledisloe Cup.

The whole affair had the effect also of cutting off relations and friendships between the New Zealand and South African unions. The outgoing chairman,

Ces Blazey, felt that the South African chairman, Danie Craven, had been duplicitous: on the one hand, saying he knew nothing about the rebel tour and, on the other, actively assisting it. Blazey's successor as chairman, Russ Thomas, wrote to Craven towards the end of the year and said: 'I covered with you the point that although you disassociated yourself with the tour, you did welcome the team to South Africa and in fact, somebody must have organised the four tests.'

CUP DAY

Thursday, 21 March 1985 was just another day for delegates to the International Rugby Board at the East India Club in St James's Square, a desirable area of Georgian buildings in central London.

There were the usual agenda items and one which had slowly made it to the front of rugby minds: the prospect of a World Cup, or international tournament as some of them called it. One of the New Zealand delegates, Ces Blazey, thought there would be support, but it would be close. South Africa's two votes would be crucial, even though there was an unspoken — unspoken at the time — acknowledgement that they would not play until the country rid itself of apartheid.

Ireland and Scotland were utterly opposed. At the other extreme were New Zealand and Australia who, as odd as it may seem, came up with the cup idea separately and, once they knew what the other was thinking, combined their efforts.

Cup ideas had been laid before the IRB previously, and firmly rejected. This time, it was an idea whose time had come, partly because it was member countries proposing it and not a commercial operator.

Australia's idea was for them to introduce the cup in their bicentenary year, 1988, but New Zealand pointed out that would clash with the Olympic Games and, if the cup were approved for every four years, lock it into the Olympic cycle. That would mean competition for sponsors, media and public attention.

So the New Zealand proposal for 1987 was agreed by the Australians and, eventually, by the IRB. Voting figures, as usual, were never made public, but it's understood the cup got approval with votes from all but Ireland and Scotland.

The Tasman neighbours set up a joint organising committee with Sir Nicholas Shehadie, the former Wallaby prop and lord mayor of Sydney, and Dick Littlejohn, a former All Blacks manager, as joint chairmen. And to keep an eye on things, the IRB set up its own cup sub-committee comprising John Kendall-Carpenter from England as chairman, Ross Turnbull from Australia, Ronnie Dawson from Ireland, Bob Stuart from New Zealand and Keith Rowlands from Wales. It was a typically compromise rugby mixture of Roundheads and Cavaliers presided over by one, Kendall-Carpenter, who had been opposed to the cup in the first place.

The Australian Rugby Union's annual report for 1985 noted the grand prize would be the Webb Ellis Trophy — subsequently named the Webb Ellis Cup, after a shadowy nineteenth-century figure who may have played football (not soccer) at Rugby School but who very few authoritative people believe had anything to do with the origins of the game.

SHIELD IN THE SUN

There surely could have been no other match like it. In 1985, Auckland went to Christchurch in search of the Ranfurly Shield. They took it away after a pulsating match in front of a crowd beyond capacity.

There were just so many elements to it. Rugby needed a day in the sun after the heavy weather of the court case that caused the intended tour of South Africa that year to be cancelled. The teams were the best two in New Zealand at the time, coached by two generally regarded as the best provincial coaches at the time, Alex Wyllie for Canterbury and John Hart for Auckland.

The demand in Auckland for tickets and flights was so great that Air New Zealand took the unprecedented step of putting Boeing 747s on their domestic route for the first time. The flights were full.

But it was even more than that. Symbolism was in the air. It was the old ways, Canterbury, against the new ways, Auckland; solidity against glitz and glamour; it was the borderland between a New Zealand we all knew and a new deregulated country we were just beginning to find out about.

And it was the end of one great shield era and the beginning of another.

Lancaster Park was packed; spectators ringed the touchline and neither police nor the modern blight on rugby, security guards, seemed to care. Marketing promotion hadn't been invented; the players were the magnet. The rugby was the thing.

At halftime, Auckland led 24–0. As the players stood around, Wyllie in his shirtsleeves walked out and told the Canterbury men that if those jokers could score twenty-four points, so could we.

A prize worthy of the game, and a game worthy of the prize.

Canterbury fought back and with just a few minutes left, trailed 23–28.

Canterbury attacked and attacked again. Wayne Smith sent an up and under soaring into the air — 40,000 pairs of eyes followed the ball. Jock Hobbs, on the side of the scrum for Canterbury, reckoned the ball seemed suspended in the air.

When it did come down in Auckland's dead-ball area, John Kirwan got fingertips to it and batted it dead. Technically, what he did was illegal. Referee Bob Francis could even have awarded a penalty try. And the shield would have stayed in Canterbury. But no one wanted the law book to ruin a day blessed by rugby gods.

The only controversy after the game was regret that the NZRFU had not allowed it to be televised live, thus denying the wider public an opportunity to see a match that had on show all the attractions of rugby to a country that has embraced it most.

WAL AND DOG

The Lions have a soft-toy lion they cart around with them and place on the touchline for games. That's a bit like the stuffed and mounted kiwi the 1924–25 All Blacks took with them on their long tour and it too appeared on the touchline and in photos.

Or later All Blacks who had 'Dog', one of the main characters in the much-loved cartoon strip, *Footrot Flats*. It wasn't just because Dog was a good Kiwi farm dog and, of course, was black and white.

His creator was a cherished New Zealand cartoonist, Murray Ball, and it was only natural that rugby was a recurring theme. Ball was steeped in the game. His father Nelson (known as Kelly) was an All Black in the 1930s and Murray himself was a fine enough midfield back to play for Manawatu, the New Zealand Juniors and in an All Blacks trial in 1959.

Long before *Footrot Flats*, Ball injected humour into a game that most New Zealanders took very seriously indeed. He did it through a book, *Fifteen Men on a Dead Man's Chest*, which covered in prose and sketches many aspects of rugby life, from rugby widows to country football to the gentlemen of the press and culminating, of course, in the test match.

He wrote and illustrated it in 1967 and dedicated it to his father and brother, Barry, who played for Wellington B. Kelly Ball went to South Africa after the war and Murray spent some school days there and recalled being jeered by the other boys when the Springboks beat the All Blacks in each of the tests in 1949. Murray worked in Britain where he developed a cartoon strip, *Stanley the Palaeolithic Hero*, which was published in *Punch* and another featuring a colonial ruffian, *Bruce the Barbarian*, published in *Labour Weekly*.

But *Footrot Flats* with Wal and Dog became his signature. The strip was so emblematic of New Zealand that the All Blacks in the early 1980s carried 'Dog' around with them, sometimes plonking him on halfway during games. There was even at least one attempt to smuggle him into an official

The last Footrot Flats *book to be published.*

team photo.

But Ball put a stop to it when the All Blacks tried to go to South Africa in 1985 and eventually went as black pirates in 1986. He said he didn't want his creation to be associated with a tour with which he personally disagreed. The players complied and Dog was dropped.

When Murray Ball died in 2017, his son Gareth recalled that *Footrot Flats* reflected the life they knew as kids. 'If we didn't see the humour in certain situations ourselves, we would certainly hear it in Dad's laughter,' he said. 'If the joke still eluded us, we would read it in a strip a week or two later.'

WOMEN'S CRUSADE

Before the Crusaders there were the Crusadettes. Quite a bit before. Before the men came the women.

A University of Canterbury women's team called the Crusadettes toured the United States and Europe in 1988 long before official rugby acknowledged that women could play the game.

The team and the tour came from the creative brain of Laurie O'Reilly, who did more for women's rugby in New Zealand than any other single person; not only did he have the organisational and persuasive influence, he also had to butt heads occasionally with male administrators who could not see past it being a men's game.

The Crusadettes played in six countries and won seventeen of twenty-one matches, scoring 520 points and conceding just sixty-seven.

One of its players, and a future Black Fern, Helen Mahon-Stroud, looked back on the tour: 'We were sleeping on floors of clubrooms. In Wales we slept on the floor of a pub. I look back at it now and you just think how crazy it was, but what it did for us in terms of our passion for the game was incredible.'

Interest in serious women's rugby — as opposed to festival games — bubbled up during the early 1980s, fostered by visits from American teams such as the Rio Grande Surfers, the Californian Kiwis and the San Diego Aztecs.

O'Reilly was a Christchurch lawyer who coached the Canterbury University men's team and women went to him for coaching advice. His involvement increased when his daughter Lauren said she wanted to play and O'Reilly declared: 'No daughter of mine will play in the front row without proper coaching.'

He became the Canterbury coach in 1985 and the first New Zealand coach in 1989. O'Reilly once wrote that he had a clear understanding with all teams with which he was involved: 'You are rugby players who happen to be women — not women who happen to be rugby players.'

The game flourished with the enthusiasm of women in Canterbury, Auckland and Taranaki and the expertise of O'Reilly. Once it had backing from national figures such as Russ Thomas, chairman of the NZRFU at the time, and J.J. Stewart, a former All Blacks coach who had become a member of the national council, it was on its way.

A first New Zealand team was chosen in 1989 and made its debut at Lancaster Park in Christchurch against an American Pacific Coast team. The New Zealanders won 13–7. A New Zealand team played in the first women's World Cup in 1990, but it was not until 1998 that the International Rugby Board gave its approval.

THEM AND US

Combining the best of New Zealand and Australia in an Anzac team has been talked about sporadically for more than a century and happened, after a fashion, in 1989.

A combined team (the name Anzac didn't exist until early 1915) was first proposed in 1899 to play Matthew Mullineaux's British team in Sydney, but the New Zealand union wasn't interested, despite moves at the time to combine the unions of New Zealand, New South Wales and Queensland, all the better to negotiate with the English union.

New South Wales, then the only active rugby state, and New Zealand wanted to go to Britain at roughly the same time in the 1920s and the English thought an Anzac team would be a good compromise. Harry Bosward, the manager of the New South Wales team in New Zealand in 1923, said at the dinner after the first 'test' in Dunedin the team for Britain should be a combined one, but the New Zealand chairman, Stan Dean, was firmly opposed.

'New Zealand is proud of her footballers and football honours and only a New Zealand team should go Home and would be pleased to meet Australia in Blighty,' he said.

A combined side was finally arranged to play the Lions in Brisbane in 1989, though it didn't really work. The match was scheduled for the Sunday between two New Zealand tests against Argentina so most of the All Blacks who were invited to Brisbane cried off. The only All Blacks test player to play against the Lions was prop Steve McDowall. The other two New Zealanders in the Anzac team were Frano Botica and Kieran Crowley, neither of them regular All Blacks at the time.

New Zealand teams playing in Australian competitions — league, soccer, basketball, baseball — is merely a modern extension of the earlier practice of the two countries combining as Australasia. Athletics, swimming and cycling all used to stage Australasian championships and an Australasian team competed at the Olympic Games in 1908 and 1912 (meaning New Zealand had a fingernail share of the rugby gold medal won by the Wallabies in 1908). New Zealand and Australia also combined as Australasia to bring the Davis Cup down under for the first time.

Plus, of course, several Australians have played for the All Blacks, and New Zealanders, for the Wallabies.

And tucked away in the Australian constitution, there still is provision for New Zealand to be added as a state.

FUTURE GLIMPSE

The All Blacks had a glimpse of rugby's commercial future when they toured Wales and Ireland in 1989 at the same time as they were forcibly reminded of the fading amateur past.

When coach Alex Wyllie and captain Wayne Shelford sat for an obligatory welcoming press conference in a function room at Heathrow, some of the first questions were about off-field engagements that had been arranged for Shelford. (But not the first question: that inquired of Wyllie how many Maori were in the team. Wyllie shrugged and turned to Shelford. 'I dunno,' he replied. 'Never counted.')

The collective of journalists, known as Fleet Street, were convinced, as they had been two years before at the first World Cup, that the All Blacks ignored the amateur regulations. Shelford had been organised to open a supermarket somewhere and this, Fleet Street argued, was professionalism. There were questions too about newspaper columns being written by players and whether they were an overt breach of the old Corinthian spirit.

An embodiment of that spirit, Bob Weighill, a man of great charm who ran the Four Home Unions, was at the press conference and he took the New Zealand manager, John Sturgeon, aside and told him the columns ought to be dropped and that while he was at it, it might be in the interests of a smooth tour to forbid players from speaking to journalists.

Sturgeon didn't stop the columns or interviews with players, but as a sop he suggested to Wyllie it might be prudent if he didn't continue his column in the *Christchurch Star*.

While all this petty poking went on, big business blithely capitalised on the All Blacks for all they were worth. A company called Schroder Unit Trusts ran a full-page colour ad in the *Daily Telegraph* that featured a colour photo of the World Cup All Blacks doing the haka and a bold headline: 'A great reputation. The outcome of years of experience.' It then went on to say how the All Blacks had worked away at their task for years and then extolled the advantages Schroder Unit Trusts had.

Another company, Bushmills Irish whiskey, ran an advertisement in national newspapers that carried a picture of All Blacks on the run and a picture of a bottle of its whiskey. One was labelled 'Black Rush' and the other 'Black Bush' and the ad asked, 'Which would you rather face?'

COMING A CROPPER

A Ranfurly Shield match between Auckland and Canterbury in 1990 had been billed as a rematch of the epic of five years before when Auckland took the shield away from Christchurch. It was Auckland's fortieth successive defence of provincial rugby's greatest prize.

But the match, rather than being another classic, turned into farce and an embarrassment for Canterbury.

After five minutes, the Canterbury hooker, John Buchan, an All Black three years before, was sent off by referee Keith Lawrence for indiscriminate rucking too close to the Auckland captain, Gary Whetton. Canterbury captain Robbie Deans and his vice-captain, Rob Penney, both pleaded with Lawrence but in vain.

Buchan, as a hooker, was able to be replaced under experimental laws at the time, and onto the field went Phil Cropper. But some of the Canterbury players told Lawrence that Cropper was a loose forward and not a hooker, and that therefore there should be no scrums, again according to the laws of the time. Lawrence had no choice but to accept the word of the Canterbury players and the match went ahead without scrums.

But there were plenty there, on the field and off, who knew that Cropper was indeed a hooker and had been played as such in the New Zealand Colts of four years before under the coaching of Brian Lochore. The other hooker in the Colts team happened to be the Auckland hooker, Sean Fitzpatrick.

It's not known what he said on the field, though it's hard to imagine him staying mum, but he made his feelings known during the week in his regular column in the newspaper, *New Truth*. He made the fair point that a front-row player ordered off could be replaced by another front-row player for safety reasons. But once it was accepted by Lawrence that Cropper was not a hooker, he should have been sent back to the reserves' bench. 'If we weren't going to have any scrums in the game then there was no reason to replace the man sent off,' Fitzpatrick wrote. 'No matter which way you look at it, it was a gutless effort from Canterbury and an embarrassment for them.'

Lindsay Knight, rugby writer and an acknowledged expert on the shield, wrote: 'Where the 1985 match will be recalled fondly as a classic . . . [this] will live on as a farce and another demonstration that all too often in rugby, because of the game's maze of rules, the law can be an ass.'

One of the Auckland props, Steve McDowall, called the match the rugby equivalent of cricket's infamous underarm incident.

BRING BACK BUCK

A sign in the crowd at the Arthur Ashe Stadium during the United States Open in the first decade of the twenty-first century was clearly visible to tennis followers and to television viewers around the world: 'Bring Back Buck', it proclaimed.

To tennis people, it would have meant nothing; to New Zealand rugby people, it meant a lot. Those three words contain a dramatic story of a great and unbeaten All Blacks captain and how, when he was no longer wanted by his coach, the country demonstrated otherwise. 'Bring Back Buck' signs popped up when he was dropped and continued to be shown years after he'd retired, as the tennis one demonstrated. (That had been taken to the tennis by a New Zealand fan who showed he had both a memory and a sense of humour.)

Buck was of course Wayne Shelford, All Black from 1985 to 1990, unbeaten test captain from 1988 to 1990; the personification of toughness and the man who, more than any other, turned the haka from a comedic ritual

Getty

A concussed Wayne Shelford (foreground) sits alongside Gary Whetton and watches the rest of the Nantes test unfold, as does coach Brian Lochore behind them.

into a respected expression of culture.

Stories followed him around. When New Zealand lost to France at Nantes in 1986 — a blessing in disguise if ever there was one — a concussed Shelford had to leave the field. It had been a brutal match. Some of the All Blacks saw just how brutal when Shelford had a shower. One of them noticed that Shelford's scrotum had been lacerated and a testicle hung down. Yet that hadn't been the reason for his leaving the field. Lesser men winced at the thought of it.

When the World Cup approached in 1987, the All Blacks decided to do a haka before each match. It had been done infrequently and inexpertly up to then. Shelford told them they had to do it properly or not at all — and he showed them how.

When Shelford led the All Blacks to Wales and Ireland in 1989, he was talismanic, a folk figure in the flesh. Players messed with him at their peril. When a Newport player tried to interfere with the All Blacks in a lineout, Shelford hit him. There was no more interference.

The next year, he was gone. There'd been rumours, all denied of course, of an Auckland clique against Shelford; there was talk he was injured, talk that he'd lost form. Whatever the cause, the effect was that Shelford the totem was gone. He played for a few lesser teams for a couple of years, then he slipped away, leaving just memories and the signs: 'Bring back Buck'.

US VERSUS THE WORLD

The All Blacks faced an unusual assignment in 1992 because of the centenary of the New Zealand union. An elite committee had been working for three years on how best to mark the milestone: it included the current chairman, Eddie Tonks, and, for some of the time, three of his predecessors, Jack Sullivan, Ces Blazey and Russ Thomas. They wanted to make the centenary memorable because other national unions such as England, Scotland, Ireland and Wales had done so, and because they knew the fiftieth anniversary had not been celebrated due to war.

They hit upon the idea of assembling a 'World XV' to play New Zealand in three matches. Although tests should only be between national entities, the committee — with the subsequent approval of the NZRFU council — decided these matches should be tests to give them the status worthy of a centenary. Consequently, a new All Blacks selection panel of Laurie Mains (coach), Earle Kirton and Peter Thorburn found themselves in the unusual position of choosing a new team to play a team they knew nothing about.

Two New Zealanders, Brian Lochore and Ivan Vodanovich, Bob Templeton of Australia and Ian McGeechan of Scotland were in charge of the selection of the World XV.

The World won the first match in

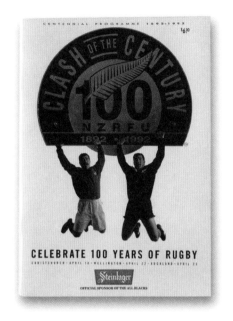

The programme for the centenary series. All Blacks prop Steve McDowall represented the 'then' and the 'now' in the haka leap.

Christchurch 28–14 so for the second in Wellington four days later, Lochore as coach made twelve changes. Another twelve were made for the third match. Another unusual aspect of the series was that for the sake of convenience or cost, the referee for the second match was Dave Bishop of Southland, the first New Zealander to referee an All Blacks' test since 1979, and the last.

The unusual nature of the series, plus the fact it was their debut, allowed the selectors to make several changes and try out combinations. The most notable absentees were the former captain, Gary Whetton, and his twin, Alan. Absent also was the probable captain, Mike Brewer, who was injured in a trial match so the leadership of the side went to Sean Fitzpatrick, who began a six-year tenure.

The All Blacks recovered from their first-test loss to beat the World XV

54–26 in Wellington and completed the series win with a 26–15 victory in Auckland against a demonstrably stronger World team. A young and promising Australian lock, John Eales, was injured in the Wellington match so he was replaced for the finale by Gary Whetton. He thus became the only New Zealander to play for the World XV and one of a handful of players to play both for and against the All Blacks.

BOKS BACK

On the morning of the end-of-isolation test against South Africa in 1992, the Afrikaans paper, *Die Burger*, devoted the whole of its front page to the match. There were photos of the two teams, a drawing of a Springbok and an All Black leaping for the ball (with the Springbok in the ascendant, naturally), and a page-width headline, 'Moordende stryd vandag'.

It translated as 'murderous battle today'. For the first time in many years of New Zealand and South Africa meeting on the rugby field, the heading referred only to the sport.

Nelson Mandela had been freed from prison two years before, negotiations for a majority rule government were proceeding, the world now looked kindly on South Africa; rugby joined in the welcoming mood with hastily arranged visits by New Zealand and Australia.

The match at Ellis Park on 15 August 1992 was the first between the two countries since 1981 in New Zealand. Speculation centred more on the South Africans because the All Blacks had been in Australia, where they had lost the series two tests to one, and had won each of their warm-up matches in South Africa against Natal, Orange Free State, the Junior Springboks and 'Central Unions', a team patched together especially for the game in Witbank (now eMalahleni) in Eastern Transvaal (Mpumalanga). The Junior Springboks the All Blacks met in Pretoria, incidentally, included a halfback that future All Blacks would get to know well, Joost van der Westhuizen.

For the test, the South Africans included two who had played in 1981, centre Danie Gerber and first five-eighth Naas Botha, who was captain. The All Blacks had no one who went back that far.

The All Blacks were expected to win, and win well, mainly because of the South Africans' isolation and their lack of international experience. That was pretty much how the match panned out, but the Springboks showed all the fire that New Zealanders had come to expect since their first meeting in 1919.

The All Blacks ushered the Springboks back into the rugby world with a 27–24 win and reading the score alone doesn't convey how the South Africans were at one stage seventeen points down and scored two tries within the last five minutes.

It was the first win at Ellis Park since the second test in 1928 and was the first time New Zealand were unbeaten in South Africa, although it was only one test. New Zealand, in the new climate, still yearned for a series win there.

THAT TRY

It was described as the try from the end of the world. That was how the French captain, Philippe Saint-André, put it. The man who scored it, Jean-Luc Sadourny, said the phrase was often used in France to describe something unexpected, something that seems to come from nowhere.

It was an apt description. It was the try that gave France a 23–20 win in the second test at Eden Park in 1994 to go with the 22–8 win from the first test in Christchurch the week before. (And with a French win in Toulouse in 1995, France moved into the rare air of teams with a hat-trick of wins against the All Blacks.)

After the win in Christchurch, Sadourny said the French feared the All Blacks would be much harder in Auckland, therefore the French effort had to be much better.

With three minutes to go, New Zealand led 20–16. It seemed enough of a margin, but the All Blacks were conscious they had not taken opportunities and should have scored more. The French knew the door had been left ajar.

One move, no mistakes. That's all it took. Saint-André caught the ball deep in the French half; a kick would have been the safest option, but it would also have given away possession. He ran infield and as he was tackled, he got the ball out to the hooker, Jean-Michel Gonzalez. He ran a bit and passed to Christophe Deylaud. The move swept to the right. Big Abdel Benazzi was there to carry it on. Then wing Émile Ntamack who changed the angle of attack, then flanker Laurent Cabannes. Deylaud handled for the second time as France approached the twenty-two, the All Blacks twisting this way and that as they tried to keep track and somehow kill the move. But there was no stopping it. Halfback Guy Accoceberry was almost at the line but just to be sure, he passed again. It went into the receptive hands of Sadourny and he dived over.

Sadourny was once asked when he knew the try was likely, when he knew that French audacity would be rewarded. 'Never,' he replied. 'I only knew for sure the try would be scored when I scored it. For me before then, there was hope and just the concentration by me and by all the French players to keep the ball and not make a mistake.'

But two wins against New Zealand, with a third to come the next year, did not mean the French thought they had an edge. The All Blacks were the yardstick, Sadourny said, and the French strived more against them 'to prove ourselves worthy of playing such a mighty team'.

THAT TACKLE

Jeff Wilson scored forty-four tries in his sixty tests, ample testimony to the majesty of his presence in the All Blacks for eight years.

But a try he didn't score gets mentioned more often than those he did. It used to gall him whenever it was brought up, and perhaps it still does even though he's well used to it. The try he didn't score was against Australia in Sydney in 1994, a try that had it been scored, would surely have won the game.

It was an odd sort of game, played on a Wednesday night at television's

Jeff Wilson almost scores . . . a moment etched in memories.

behest to avoid a timing clash with the opening of the Commonwealth Games in Victoria, Canada. It was also the first time the Bledisloe Cup had been at stake in a night match.

The cup seemed destined for Wallaby hands almost from the opening seconds because Jason Little scored, then Phil Kearns scored after about twenty-five minutes and at halftime, Australia led 17–6.

Slowly, the All Blacks got back into the match and, privately, some of them afterwards said they were confident they had the better of the Wallabies and the points would come. But they didn't come quickly enough or often enough, or in sufficient quantity. Michael Jones seemed headed for the goal-line, but referee Ed Morrison had seen a forward pass. Down to the last minutes. Australia ahead 20–16.

Wilson, who had made his debut the year before but had not been wanted for the earlier tests of 1994, got the ball about thirty-five metres out. In that long-striding lope of his, blond hair flopping, he beat flanker David Wilson.

Then he beat another David, Campese. The line was near, Shane Howarth was there in case he was needed.

Wilson was in the act of diving for the line when 21-year-old George Gregan, playing his first test against New Zealand, pounced like a thief in the night. Somehow, by accident or design, he managed to tackle Wilson and at the same time jolt the ball out of his arms. The moment was lost, the test was lost.

Wilson had seen Gregan in his peripheral vision but thought he could still score. But alas. Inevitably, though a game of eighty-odd minutes, attention was on the last one or two. Moments in a game that affect the outcome can happen at any time, not just in the last minute. But that's always where the focus is.

Wilson was devastated. So were the other All Blacks. That's what a loss does. As Wilson would be the first to say, he didn't need constant reminding of it.

CHAIRMAN RUSS

Russ Thomas was one of the few administrators who saw the value of amateurism at the same time as he saw the inevitability of professionalism; he came from an age of trust and love of the game and moved into one of contracts and legal fees and individuals before the game.

He was the last of the romantics. Thomas knew what he was talking about in both eras; amateur to the core, he was chief executive of the Foodstuffs company in the South Island. He knew big business before rugby itself became big business.

Thomas joined the New Zealand union in the early 1970s as one of a new guard, one of those who hadn't been adult during the Second World War, one with fresh ideas. He left it twenty years later despairing national administrators had lost touch with the grass roots and worried that players put themselves above the game.

Thomas's rise to national acclaim had come through being manager of the 1978 and 1979 All Blacks and in the mid-80s, he succeeded Ces Blazey as chairman. A keen advocate of the World Cup, he became chairman of the cup organising committee.

Along the way, his love of the game was never threatened, but his faith in it was. He was personally shaken when he saw during the Cavaliers debacle how disloyal players could be and shattered that some personally lied to him. His faith was dealt another blow in 1990 when he was ousted as chairman in a ballot, rather than being given the courtesy of stepping down at his moment of choosing.

When he eventually stood down in 1994, he made a telling comment: 'We must never lose sight of the grass roots and if I have any regrets about the way New Zealand rugby is heading, it is that we now talk a lot about money and not enough about the game.'

Russ Thomas as Rugby World Cup Ltd chairman.

There was nothing hidden about Thomas. What he felt, he said. He had a line about 'this great game of rugby football, preserving it for our children and our children's children'. While those who had heard it often could smile indulgently, they also knew he meant every word of it.

It was this regard for the game that led him, courageously, to stand at a gathering of British administrators and tell them that if they continued to run the game as they were, it would be destroyed. Visiting 'colonials' were not expected to speak so honestly.

LOMU ARRIVES

The value of tries rests in the ears and eyes of the beholder. A sensational try to one person is just another try to someone else. Gareth Edwards' try for the Barbarians against New Zealand in 1973 is often described as the greatest try of all time — usually by people in the northern hemisphere. Nationalism determines judgement.

Unique. Lomu over and through Mike Catt.

But here's one try that the rugby world hasn't stopped talking about. It came when the All Blacks played England in the World Cup semifinal at Newlands in Cape Town in 1995. It was the first try of the game and it set the tone for what happened — a whopping 45–29 towelling of an England side that had been riding high on confidence.

Andrew Mehrtens' kick-off found some free space out among the England backs and when they tried to gather, it was knocked on. From the scrum, the ball went right to Jeff Wilson, but he suddenly switched play to the left. England's defenders scrambled this way and that.

Jonah Lomu, whom the All Blacks planned to get into play as soon as possible, found himself with the ball. Lomu related his thoughts in the book he did with Warren Adler: 'Look out, here's Underwood coming in for the hit. Misses. Spins. Goal-line ahead. Not far now. Around the outside of Carling. Damn, he's clipped me. Stumbling. Keep your balance, Jonah. . . . Look up. Mike Catt. Two strides. No option. Shoulder in my vision. Get your knee up, Jonah. Bang. Into him. Over him. Through him . . . sorry, Mike.'

Three more tries went Lomu's way that day. It was Lomu at his thundering best, Lomu the most extraordinary rugby player to take the field. New Zealanders saw him coming — right from when he was a Gulliver among schoolboy Lilliputians, usually playing at No. 8 or flanker. Then there was his tentative test debut against France in 1994; a bit unsure, a bit lost in a losing All Blacks team.

Once was lost, now am found. The World Cup showed New Zealanders a different Lomu, a prepared Lomu, a fearsome Lomu. And the rest of the world, for the first time, realised what a unique player he was.

And if people in England didn't see on television how comprehensively the cream of their rugby turned sour, they could read *The Times* on the Monday morning: 'Lomu runs England ragged'. And the opening sentence from veteran reporter David Hands: 'And when they awoke from their nightmare, England found it was all true.'

FOLLOW THE MONEY

No day had more significance in rugby than 27 August 1995. That was the day, a Sunday in Paris, that the International Rugby Board overturned its guiding principle and declared the game to be open: anyone could be paid for playing.

It came a neat century, coincidentally, after another day of great importance to the game, when clubs in England's northern counties walked away from the English union over several issues, money just one of them, and formed league.

The word 'revolution' was in the air in 1995. French federation president Bernard Lapasset declared the change to money was a revolution. But it wasn't. It was evolution; it was inevitable.

Rugby league had newly acquired riches from news media tycoon Rupert Murdoch and its clubs were targeting rugby like never before as they sought to position themselves in the 'war' between Murdoch's proposed 'Super League' and the established Australian Rugby League competition. The three main southern hemisphere countries, New Zealand, Australia and South Africa, went to league's source, Murdoch, for money with which to counter the threat. From out of the scrum of confusion came a former Australian prop, Ross Turnbull, with a plan for a professional rugby competition. Amateur players were faced with riches from a game they played for nothing.

The nineteenth-century Corinthian ethic of amateurism had been under strain in recent years; now it was at breaking point. Faced with these threats, the IRB had little choice but to sell the soul it had clung to for a century. It had to adopt what most people saw as the only choice for the future or be trapped in an impractical past.

All that surprised was the completeness of the change. The IRB met for its momentous decision in the Hotel Ambassador on Boulevard Haussmann in the classy shopping district of Paris. In the amateur days, most players wouldn't have been able to afford a drink there. Now, some players could probably buy it.

Not everyone welcomed the IRB's capitulation. Roger Uttley, a former England player and coach, described 27 August 1995 as the day fun went out of the game.

(Seventeen days before the IRB jumped across its Rubicon, Jeff Wilson and Josh Kronfeld became the first All Blacks to sign player contracts with the NZRFU; the others had been holding out for Turnbull's promised riches.) Over the next few weeks, the New Zealand union was able to sign most of its current All Blacks and other leading players. Only a few went to league.

As it was the NZRFU that had the money, it was the body that contracted the players. It meant the All Blacks would always have first call on players' services. Rugby elsewhere went down a different route because of different structures and followed the path mapped out by soccer years before. The conflict of country versus club became a recurring problem for the game.

LE BOMBE

When the former French president, Jacques Chirac, died in 2019, an obituary in an Australian think tank's newsletter said that Jonah Lomu had once threatened to place explosives in Chirac's garden.

Somehow, *The Interpreter*, the newsletter of the Lowy Institute, misinterpreted. Lomu did say something like that, but not quite those words or with that meaning.

Lomu late in 1995 was on the All Blacks' tour of Italy and France and he, and a few of his teammates, including captain Sean Fitzpatrick, wrote to Chirac, who was then in his first year as president, complaining about French nuclear testing in the South Pacific.

Lomu began his letter by saying he had considered not touring France because of opposition to nuclear testing 'but then I decided that it is not the people of France that I have anything against, it is the people who decided to explode nuclear bombs in my Pacific Backyard . . .'.

He said in his typed letter that Chirac had helped with his motivation — 'hopefully we will be able to show you a few explosions of our own in your backyard, Explosions of Pacific Power on the rugby field'.

Each of the players wrote their own letters and fired them off together to the Élysée Palace. It's not known if Chirac acknowledged them or even read them; although a fluent English speaker, he was well known for refusing to speak English.

Josh Kronfeld, a flanker on the tour though he didn't play because of injury, had famously worn headgear during the New Zealand domestic season with the 'ban the bomb' symbol drawn on it.

Representatives of about thirty organisations also protesting about French nuclear testing assembled outside the All Blacks' hotel in Nancy in the last week of the tour. The group, representing ginger organisations such as Greenpeace, Women Against War and 'Les Verts' (the Greens), stood outside the hotel entrance, displaying placards and banners, before they were moved on by police.

Emma Jones, an Aucklander teaching English in Nancy, was interpreter and spokeswoman. 'There's united opposition in France to the testing,' she said, 'and the groups got together to make sure the All Blacks . . . understand that.'

All Blacks Jeff Wilson, Michael and Ian Jones and Robin Brooke spoke to the protesters outside the hotel and were given dove badges and origami cranes, the latter symbolising the atomic bombing of Hiroshima at the end of the Second World War.

Chirac stopped France's underground nuclear testing programme the following year.

President Chirac

I thought seriously about not coming to France because of my personal feelings against nuclear testing, particularly in the Pacific.

But then I decided that it is not the people of France that I have anything against, it is the people who decided to explode nuclear bombs in my Pacific Backyard , and they definitely appear to be in the minority.

I am proud to be a New Zealander but I am also very proud of my Pacific heritage and I am angry that a group of politicians, scientists and military men have decided to conduct their nuclear experiments in a part of the world that is very important to me.

For the next few weeks you have certainly helped me with my motivation, hopefully we will be able to show you a few explosions of our own in your backyard

Explosions of Pacific Power on the rugby field.

Jonah Lomu

Jonah Lomu's letter of protest to the French president.

AT LAST

It was the first full year of professional rugby but most of all, it was the year in which New Zealand finally laid the South African bogey to rest. If 1996 was going to be typical of the brave new world of professional rugby, New Zealanders wanted more of it.

The All Blacks' visit to South Africa was in two parts. The first was a test at Newlands in Cape Town that was the last of the new Tri Nations series. A separate test series began the week after that, pitting the All Blacks against their most formidable foe in Durban, Pretoria and Johannesburg. The All Blacks gained the early points in Durban and led 15–3 after the first twenty minutes, but they could never claim dominance. It was as hard a test as any between these two countries. The South Africans fought back but were never able to gain the lead. The All Blacks' 23–19 win was generally seen as deserved but the real significance was that it put New Zealand one up.

Their faces tell the story: Sean Fitzpatrick had just captained, and John Hart coached, New Zealand to a first series victory in South Africa.

The showdown came at Loftus Versfeld in Pretoria, a ground that is almost Fort Afrikaner, one in which the crowds bay for the blood of those who don't call the place home. It's one of those grounds where the crowd is as much opposition as the players on the field.

The All Blacks beat both on a never-to-be-forgotten day. This was what New Zealand rugby people had been wanting since 1928; this was what they considered they had been cheated out of on at least two occasions. This, the chance to beat South Africa on their own grounds, was what motivated and sustained some New Zealanders through the apartheid years.

Finally, in the legitimacy of the new South Africa, New Zealand achieved its aim. The 33–26 win in the second test in Pretoria, three tries each, was memorable not for how it was played, not for any incidents in the game, not for individual brilliance (of which there was much), but for just the outcome. For the first time, the All Blacks beat the Springboks in a series in South Africa.

In New Zealand, grown men cried. In Pretoria, grown men cried. Don Clarke, the fullback who had strived so much to beat South Africa and then gone to spend his life there, sat under the stand and wept his tears of joy. So did other All Blacks of other eras.

The final test at Ellis Park was almost an anticlimax and the Springboks won 32–22. The better team won the third test; but the better team won the series. New Zealand was content.

A DYNASTY BUILT

Rugby entered a brave new world in 1996 with Super 12 and the Tri Nations as its professional flagships. In that first year, as the public tried to get used to regional teams elbowing in ahead of the time-honoured provincial rep teams, the Canterbury Crusaders finished stone motherless last, to use the expressive phrase racing commentators used to like.

Coached by Vance Stewart and captained by Richard Loe, the Crusaders managed only two wins, at home against New South Wales and away — in New Plymouth — against the Hurricanes. The following year, with Wayne Smith as coach and Todd Blackadder as captain, they finished mid-table. And then came 1998. They beat the Sharks from Durban at home in a semifinal and went on to Eden Park to beat the defending champions, the Blues. They had their first title.

The following year, 1999, they went south for the final to Carisbrook, where they beat the Highlanders to be champions for a second successive year, then another title the following year. By then, Wayne Smith had moved on to the All Blacks and Robbie Deans had taken over as coach.

The Crusaders' dynasty of accomplishment had been established. In the formative years of Super Rugby, the chief executive of the host union was also the boss of the Super team. Critical to the rise and rise of the Crusaders was the Canterbury board's decision to hire a young and promising administrator called Steve Tew, then in his early thirties, from the Hillary Commission. Tew, with

The first of many ... Wayne Smith and Todd Blackadder after the 1998 Super 12 final.

Deans and Blackadder and others for whom red and black were the colours of success, built not just a successful team year by year but also a succession plan. When it was time for one player to move on, there was another waiting to move in. It became almost seamless. Andrew Mehrtens to Daniel Carter . . . Scott Robertson to Richie McCaw . . . Leon MacDonald to Ben Blair . . .

The Crusaders became the benchmark for New Zealand rugby success. They won ten titles from 1998 to 2019 and were beaten finalists four times. Even in the year in which their city was devastated by earthquake and they didn't have a home ground any more, they still finished runner-up.

When the great teams of New Zealand rugby are talked about, Hawke's Bay of the 1920s, Otago of the 1940s, Auckland of the 1960s and 1980s, the Crusaders deserve to be at the front of the sentence.

ANNUS HORRIBILIS

Every so often the All Blacks have an aberrant year, one that is at odds with the enduring record. One such year was 1949, when six tests were lost (by two different test teams); another equally black and bleak year was 1998, the worst since 1949.

The year began with some promise, even though it was against an England team much removed from the strongest possible line-up because clubs in England asserted their financial whiphand. The All Blacks as a result were expected to dominate in the two tests, the first in Dunedin and the second in Auckland. They did, winning the first 64–22 and the second 40–10, but there was an air of dissatisfaction.

The All Blacks, captained for the first time by Taine Randell, went to Melbourne for the first of the Tri Nations tests. It was not a trip of happy memories. It became the All Blacks' first loss in the Tri Nations, their first since 1996 and their first loss in Australia since 1994. The Wallabies' fullback, Matt Burke, scored all of Australia's twenty-four points from two tries, a conversion and four penalty goals.

It was the most points by anyone in a test against New Zealand.

Things did not improve for New Zealand in Wellington for the fiftieth test match against South Africa. The Springboks won 13–3, the first time the All Blacks had been held to such a paltry score since the infamous loss to France in 1986 and the first time at home since the loss to the Lions in Wellington in 1971. The hole just got deeper the following week when the Wallabies won in New Zealand for the first time since 1990 and, remarkably, their first win in Christchurch for forty years. The win also gave the Australians the Bledisloe Cup for the first time since 1994.

The return match against South Africa in Durban was a better New Zealand performance, and by halftime, New Zealand had a 17–5 lead. But, inevitably, the Springboks were not done and with a minute or so to go, the All Blacks led by four points. South Africa drove for the line and referee Peter Marshall pointed to hooker James Dalton and signalled a try. The conversion missed, but who cared? The All Blacks had lost by a point.

The last match of the year was another loss, this time 19–14 to Australia in Sydney. The Wallabies beat the All Blacks three times in the one year for the first time since 1929. The All Blacks lost five in a row, their worst record. Yes, New Zealand lost six in a row in 1949, but that was by two different teams: the top thirty Pakeha players were in South Africa and they lost four and the second-string New Zealanders (including Maori who weren't second string) lost two official tests against Australia. So the 1998 record was worse.

AN UNMATCHABLE MAN

Brian Lochore was a towering figure in New Zealand rugby. He was a big man with a personality to match. An All Black from 1963 until 1970 and captain in a five-year unbeaten era, he also coached the All Blacks to win the first World Cup in 1987 and in his last years, he was patron of the New Zealand Rugby Union.

It seemed at times the All Blacks couldn't do without him. In 1995, nearly

Getty

Sir Brian Lochore

a decade after he'd stopped coaching, he was called back to the colours to be campaign manager in the 1995 World Cup. And nearly a decade after that, he was called back once again to be a selector.

But it wasn't just rugby. Lochore was much respected in the farming community for the excellence of his common-sense views which had the core value of matching the best possible farming methods with the best possible care and use of the land.

Lochore once said ruefully that he found it difficult to say no, especially when he was asked to do something for his country. He worked voluntarily for the sports-funding body, the Sports Foundation, giving grants to athletes who could not otherwise afford to compete overseas; and he succeeded his old captain, Wilson Whineray, as chairman of the Hillary Commission, the overarching sports body that preceded Sport New Zealand. From netball to education, Lochore contributed when he was asked. Different governments rewarded him with a knighthood and the ultimate honour, membership of the numerically restricted Order of New Zealand.

One of the enduring stories of his sense of duty was how in 1971, when he was in his first year of retirement from the All Blacks, he received a call at his Wairarapa farm to play in the third test against the Lions because lock Peter Whiting was injured and captain Colin Meads, a dear Lochore friend, was in doubt. Lochore didn't hesitate and headed south, but not before writing a note for his wife Pam and leaving it on the kitchen table: 'Gone to Wellington to play in test. Will ring later. Love. BJ.'

To most New Zealanders, Lochore was a famous name, not seen often on television in his playing days but instantly recognisable, nevertheless. To family and friends, Lochore was no different to the image the wider public had: deeply loyal with a profound sense of duty, a ready smile and a quick wit (often at his own expense). He had friends throughout New Zealand and when he and Pam travelled, he made sure he called in to say hello.

He was, as someone said at his funeral at his beloved Memorial Oval in Masterton, 'a good bugger'. Praise can come no higher.

AN UNFORGETTABLE TEST

Every so often, there's a test match that takes the breath away. One of this rare type happened in Sydney in 2000. The Australians were at a formidable height in their history and they had, after all, become the first country to win the World Cup twice. They had a group of outstanding players led by the most outstanding of them all, John Eales.

The test at Stadium Australia, into which an improbably precise total of 109,878 people crammed, was one of those tests that people still talked about years after the final whistle.

Within eight minutes of the start, the All Blacks were up 24–0. Tana Umaga scored in the first minute, then Pita Alatini in the third and Christian Cullen in the fifth. Andrew Mehrtens converted each of them and added a penalty goal.

Most sides hammered by such an early scoring blitz would be destroyed, incapable of counter-attack, and would concentrate more on limiting any further damage. But the Wallabies were not most sides. Incredibly, within half an hour Stirling Mortlock had scored twice and Chris Latham and Joe Roff once. Mortlock had also kicked two conversions so when referee Andre Watson blew for halftime, giving himself and everyone else some relief, the score was 24-all.

The second half was more orthodox, although only by comparison with the first. It was still played at high speed and with a competitive ferocity that only the best teams in the world can maintain for any length of time. It was a game that transfixed all who saw it, and it went by in a blur for the players.

There were more tries, more penalty goals, and with six minutes to go, Hamilton-born Jeremy Paul scored to make the score 35–34 to Australia. The All Blacks seemed to increase the intensity as they sought a score to take the lead in the twilight minutes.

It seemed that everyone in the crowd, as massive as it was, was on their feet, roaring for black or for gold. The noise was colossal, the tension enormous, the occasion magnificent.

The All Blacks attacked the Australian line one more time. The ball came back and went to Taine Randell, standing about fifteen metres out. His passage was blocked. So too was any chance of an orthodox pass. But outside him on

Stephen Larkham lunges, but in vain. Jonah Lomu on his way to the winning try.

the touchline was Jonah Lomu. Randell lobbed the ball out to him, Lomu caught it and charged. Stephen Larkham got a hand on him, but it would have taken more than a hand to stop Lomu so close to the line.

The All Blacks won a match people swore they would never forget. Nick Farr-Jones, a thinking halfback in his day, reckoned it was the greatest test match of all time. Not many would have disagreed.

UNWANTED ATTENTION

Spectators have occasionally invaded the rhythm of a test match, even if they only went by the name of streakers and flopped around briefly somewhere near the touchline.

But in Durban in 2002, in yet another drumhead-tight test match between New Zealand and South Africa, it was something altogether different. Something similar may have happened before in the 130 or so years of test rugby, but not before a frenzied crowd of 52,000 and millions of television viewers.

Early in the second half, the score was 17-all. South Africa could have been in front but wing Breyton Paulse had been denied what seemed a legitimate try by the Irish referee, David McHugh. All reports of the match said how hot it was at Kings Park that day; heat and the rising tension of the match frayed nerves.

It all snapped for one burly spectator, Pieter van Zyl. Clad in a South African jersey and jeans, he lumbered on to the ground with the seeming intent of doing harm to McHugh.

Richie McCaw was playing in his ninth test and his first in Durban. He recalled the day: 'All I saw coming was a green jersey . . . then bang, the ref . . . crashed into me.' His first thought was that one of the South African players had done the unthinkable and attacked McHugh.

McCaw and others hauled van Zyl out the way and wrestled him to the ground, van Zyl gaining a bloodied nose in the process. McCaw said he wasn't responsible for that. 'There's a photo floating around of me with my fist cocked and it appears as if I'm about to hit the bloke. Truth is, I never threw a punch.

Getty

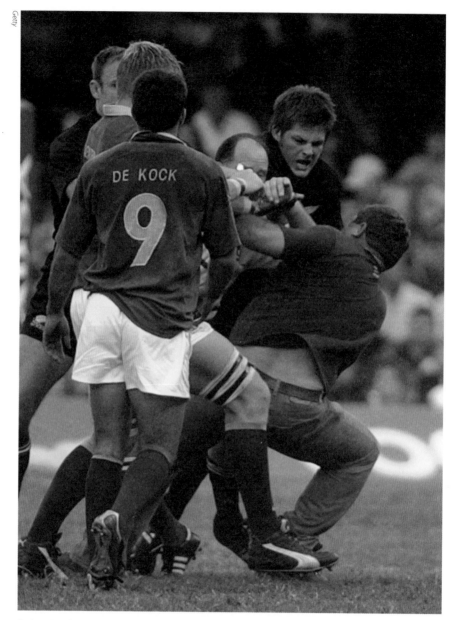

Richie McCaw assists in the rescue of referee David McHugh.

It was one of the big Bok boys who got a few in and did a bit of damage.'

Van Zyl, a 42-year-old mining engineer from Potchefstroom, about 600 km north and west of Durban, was defiant and unrepentant afterward. Told he'd be charged with causing grievous bodily harm, he responded: 'Don't forget that the incident happened when the referee closed his one eye and ceased to see the Springboks.' Van Zyl eventually pleaded guilty to common assault, was convicted and fined 10,000 rand (about $NZ1000), and banned for life from any grounds controlled by the South African union.

McHugh had a shoulder dislocated, caused by some of the players trying to drag him out of harm's way. He had to be replaced for the remaining half an hour of the game by a touch judge, Chris White of England.

The All Blacks broke the deadlock and won 30–23.

SOUR RELATIONS

Relations between rugby authorities in New Zealand and the world governing body, then known as the International Rugby Board, reached their lowest point in the early years of the twenty-first century.

The issue was whether New Zealand could or should host some of the games in the 2003 World Cup, which was being played mainly in Australia. The Australians and the IRB had agreed to the sub-host role, as it was called, but nothing appeared to progress smoothly.

New Zealand was scheduled to host two pools, two quarterfinals and a semifinal, and the Australian union agreed to limit any New Zealand losses.

But there was New Zealand reluctance to go ahead because of the cup's impact on provincial matches, because of the potential for loss, and because of the World Cup body's insistence on 'clean' grounds; that is, grounds totally free of advertising and commercial names.

The continuing wrangling was not helped by the IRB chairman, Vernon Pugh, a Welsh lawyer, virtually running the organisation on his own. The IRB at the time had not had a chief executive for several months and the New

Zealand chairman, Murray McCaw, said Pugh had too much power.

Such was the low state of relations, the NZRFU discussed privately the possibility of not playing in the cup, never mind part-hosting it.

In the end, the Rugby World Cup company recommended to its parent body, the IRB, that Australia host the cup on its own. The IRB said: 'Generous accommodation made by RCWL [Rugby World Cup Ltd] to meet the needs and problems of the NZRU were repaid with consistent failures and wholly inappropriate behaviour.'

A retired chief justice, Sir Thomas Eichelbaum, appointed by the NZRFU as a one-man inquiry, found the union adopted a cautious approach; 'it created the impression that it did not properly value the cup and there was a breakdown in relations between the principal parties'.

As a result, McCaw and the chief executive, David Rutherford, resigned and at the insistence of provincial unions, all board members also resigned. A special general meeting of the union elected five new members. One of them, Jock Hobbs, a former All Blacks captain and member of the preceding NZRFU council, became chairman.

By the end of the year, Chris Moller, deputy chief executive of Fonterra, the dairy co-operative, became chief executive. Within a few years, Hobbs and Moller together spearheaded the successful bid for New Zealand to stage the World Cup in 2011.

(Vernon Pugh died in 2003, just a few months before the World Cup that Australia hosted alone.)

CREATE THE WIND

Some players sniff the wind, others create it. That was once a line from the great Lions coach of 1971, Carwyn James. 'It is the flyhalf's role,' he went on, 'to give form, dextrously and imaginatively, to his team's movement.'

Flyhalf, out-half, first five-eighth, it's all the same. Even 'the 10' to use the modern jargon. James didn't live to see Dan Carter play at first five-eighth for

New Zealand against the Lions in Wellington in the second test in 2005, but Carter fulfilled the James ideal.

Few players at any period of rugby have dominated a single test match as did Carter on the night of 2 July 2005, when the Lions aimed to square the three-match series after losing the first in the wind and rain of Christchurch the week before. Their coach, Clive Woodward, gambled heavily on becoming the second Lions coach (after James) to win a series in New Zealand. He gambled and lost.

Carter in Wellington scored thirty-three of the All Blacks' forty-eight points, a remarkable feat in itself. It was the third highest tally by an individual in a test; Simon Culhane had scored forty-five against Japan in 1995, Tony Brown thirty-six against Italy in 1999, then Carlos Spencer and Andrew Mehrtens,

Dan Carter scores his second try against the Lions in Christchurch.

both with thirty-three in matches in 1997 (against Argentina and Ireland).

But this was against the Lions, a team chosen with meticulous attention to detail with the express purpose of beating New Zealand in a series. And here was Carter, treating the hand-picked best of British and Irish with a lordly display of accomplished skill. There could have been no better example of the perfect execution of the rugby player's art.

Carter scored two tries and kicked goals from all over the place, but it was more than that. It was where he positioned himself to take passes from Byron Kelleher and Justin Marshall, how he read the pattern of play and could see a move or two ahead of anyone else, how he could spy a gap that was beyond the ken of anyone else. Carter would have many more fine games for New Zealand, but none approaching this for complete control.

His two tries were a combination of sleight of foot as well as hand; the one chipping and chasing down a touchline, turning his opponents inside out as they watched, turned, ran and winced. The other was more orthodox, just a glide through a backline when there was no right for there to be room.

If James could but have seen, this was a night when Carter created the wind.

DARKNESS IN CARDIFF

The All Blacks have had darker days than 7 October 2007; it just didn't seem so at the time, or for some people, for several years to come. That was the day when New Zealand were beaten 20–18 in a World Cup quarterfinal by France.

It was a devastating loss, the All Blacks' earliest exit from the tournament that had come to dominate international rugby.

Would they ever win the World Cup again? That seemed to be the anguished question up and down the land that became the land of the long black cloud. The cup in 2007 was supposed to make up for the loss in 2003, which was itself supposed to make up for the loss in 1999. Those two were at least sei-finals.

There was despondency and there was anger in the Millennium Stadium after the game and, almost inevitably, the referee got the blame. He was 28-year-old Wayne Barnes, a London solicitor who had refereed his first test just the year before. He was young and inexperienced by cup standards. And most damning of all, he missed a forward pass by Frédéric Michalak that led to a try by Yannick Jauzion. It could have made all the difference, but such things happen in rugby. The fault, dear Brutus . . .

France were sometimes the France of old; the quick passing and incisive running. They faced the haka wearing a mix of red, white and blue T-shirts and managed to form up in a fair facsimile of the French flag.

And perhaps the All Blacks, after an untroubled gallop through pool play against Italy, Portugal, Scotland and Romania, subconsciously took it all a wee

Brendon Leonard dives, but Frédéric Michalak runs. World Cup quarterfinal, 2007.

bit lightly. How else to explain the non-selection of two of the backline leaders, Aaron Mauger and Doug Howlett?

Some of the players were in tears after the game, a despair born of knowledge that they were good enough to win, should have been good enough to win, but didn't. The chairman of the New Zealand union, Jock Hobbs, was furious but was able to resist for the most part the blaming of the referee.

A few weeks after the match, Hobbs was a solemn figure at the union's player awards dinner, a celebration that was as flat as the champagne that remained untouched. Coincidentally, it was during this dinner that Hobbs's brother-in-law, Robbie Deans, negotiated his way out of the Crusaders and into the arms of the Wallabies. To some surprise, the losing coach, Graham Henry, was reappointed to have another crack at a cup that had proved to be so captivatingly elusive.

THE LAST OF LOMU

In the northern hemisphere winter of 2009–10, Germany prepared for the FIFA World Cup for some of the time in Sicily, a nice sun-drenched place to get away from the northern European winter.

Also on the island at the time was a French third-division rugby team, Vitrolles Marseilles. The two teams got together a bit, footballers of different shapes, had a run or two and probably a beer or two.

Jonah Lomu was there. He delighted in putting the Germans through some lineout moves. Lomu then was playing at No. 8, back in the position where it had all begun for him so many years before. He was then thirty-four, making his last, sad but bold attempt at a rugby comeback.

A world superstar, a name known round the world, now plying his trade in a semi-professional league that few watched or even knew about. But that was Lomu. A weakened body, but he remained a lionheart.

By then, his kidney transplant that prolonged his life had been nearly six years before. After headlining in two World Cups, in 1995 and 1999, he made one last desperate attempt to play in a third, in 2003, but his body wasn't up to it. Remarkably, the kidney disease that blighted his life and hastened its end was known only to a few confidants during his barnstorming run at the top.

Just as remarkably, he returned to rugby after the transplant, playing for Cardiff and North Harbour as well as occasional charity or other fundraising matches: his form and fitness wasn't what it had been at his peak, but his name was as magnetic as ever.

The move to the south of France was one last attempt to revive a career that he must have known could not be revived. He loved the lifestyle and tried the language though found that in games the French talked too fast for him and sometimes he didn't know what was going on.

For his first game, against the Montmelian team from the Alps, about a hundred reporters showed up with the crowd of about 2500. Lomu played at centre. It was a game that didn't mean much, except to Lomu. 'He was incredibly motivated,' coach Alain Hyardet recalled. 'I explained to him it was only third division. . . . I then understood what this match meant to him . . . he could finally play rugby again . . . it was like a new birth.' He played a few more games, then called a quiet halt to the most extraordinary career the game has seen.

DOCTORS' FIRST XV

That august organ of the medical profession, the *British Medical Journal*, usually fills its pages with articles of a highly technical nature with language that leaves lay people behind. A heading that says 'Low molecular weight heparin does not prevent VTE after knee arthroscopy, studies show' is not likely to attract the casual reader.

The occasional rugby stories in the *BMJ*, as with other medical journals, are usually about injury and treatment and written by and for clinicians. But in 2010, with the World Cup in New Zealand edging closer, the *BMJ* dropped its academic cloak.

Three researchers in Auckland, Yu-Mwee Tan, Andrew Connolly and

Andrew Hill, set out to identify men who were both successful in their medical careers and in rugby. They came up with 150 candidates, the majority of whom had played for their universities. They found twenty-eight who had played for either New Zealand or New Zealand Maori. Then came the difficult bit. They named their First XV, based purely on rugby ability. All Blacks were given preference for each position if more than one candidate was eligible.

Their Doctors' First XV (All Blacks dates unless otherwise noted):

Fullback: Tony Davies (1960–62)
Right wing: Russell Watt (1957–58, 60–62)
Centre: Jeremy Stanley (1997)
Second five-eighth: Ron Elvidge (1946, 49–50)
Left wing: Graham Moore (1949)
First five-eighth: Billy Fea (1921)
Halfback: David Kirk (1983–87)
No. 8: Hugh Burry (1960)
Flankers: David Dickson (1925), Des Oliver (1953–54)
Locks: Lawrie Knight (1974, 76–77), Ian Prior (Otago 1941–44)
Props: Geoffrey Gordon (Canterbury, Otago 1942–46), Mark Irwin (1955–56, 58–60)
Hooker: Nicholas Mantell (Auckland 1991–92, Waikato 1997–99)
Reserves: Don Macpherson (1905), Peter Tapsell (Otago 1953), Jimmy Sinclair (1923), Arnold Perry (1923), Donald Stevenson (1926), Kevin O'Connor (Otago 1945–49), Manahi ('Doc') Paewai (Otago 1940–43, Auckland 1944, Wellington 1946, North Auckland 1947, 50–52).

The authors acknowledged selection of the captain would provoke debate, but they went for Elvidge, based on his skills and anecdotes about his leadership, over Kirk, more widely known because of his World Cup captaincy.

The authors noted the obvious feature — a distinct lack of modern player-doctors; only Kirk from the 1980s and only Stanley from the professional era.

THE CUP AT LAST

When the French players formed themselves into a V formation to confront the haka before the Word Cup final in 2011, knowledgeable spectators knew they were seeing something special.

V for victory; a symbolic echo of the Second World War when the opening bars of Beethoven's Fifth Symphony sounded the Allies' intentions — in Morse, dit-dit-dit-dah, V for victory. On this occasion, the V indicated French intentions.

And they were nearly fulfilled. The final score of 8–7 reflected the determination and desperation of both teams: New Zealand's need to win the cup for a second time and lay to rest the demons of the past; France's great desire to win the cup for a first time.

New Zealand led 5–0 at halftime and such a margin usually counts for nothing in modern rugby but in this game, it counted for a lot. For a long time,

Success at last . . . Richie McCaw and his All Blacks, 2011.

Tony Woodcock's try seemed to be enough. The All Blacks had had chances with kicks at goal, but it was Piri Weepu's responsibility that night, and the kicks did not go over. Another kicker, Aaron Cruden, went down with injury and then came a saviour of sorts, Stephen Donald, fourth choice as first five-eighth. He extended the lead to 8–0 with a penalty goal soon after halftime.

It then became a matter of defence. Time and again the French thrust at the All Blacks' line, like a bull butting an enclosing fence. Time and again, the fence in the form of the All Blacks held. Just once was there a breach and the French captain, Thierry Dusautoir, thundered over by the posts. François Trinh-Duc, France's replacement first-five of Vietnamese descent, kicked the conversion as easy as you like.

With a point in it, the pressure on New Zealand intensified. The drama at Eden Park enveloped the nation. Could the All Blacks hold? Could France contrive one more score? The answers were yes and no. Rugby's a team game and it was the twenty New Zealanders in black who held out and won the cup for the second time. But if one stood out above the rest, the high peak of a mountain range, it was Richie McCaw, the captain. Statistics somewhere probably say how many tackles he made, but it wasn't the number that counted, it was where they were made and how significant they were when they were made. One for certain stopped a try by the French wing, Alexis Palisson.

It was the All Blacks' second World Cup win, but it was Richie McCaw's night. There could have been no more fitting finale to the work on and off the field to reach this climax on this night.

TOUCHING TRIBUTE

Jerry Collins, a hard-tackling flanker or No. 8, was part of two unsuccessful World Cup campaigns. He played in the semifinal loss to Australia in 2003 and in the quarterfinal loss to France in 2007. By 2011, Collins was playing in Wales for Ospreys.

By the time of the next cup, in 2015, he was dead. He and his partner Alana

Madill died in a car crash in southern France in June 2015, four months before the All Blacks won the cup again, beating Australia in the final at Twickenham.

His former teammates had not forgotten him. A few days later, in a touching gesture, some of them took the cup out to Collins's grave at the Whenua Tapu cemetery north of Wellington. They paid their tribute the day before a welcome home parade in Wellington and the day after what would have been Collins's thirty-fifth birthday. No journalists or camera crews were present and it became public only through the players' own posts on social media.

Ma'a Nonu, who played with Collins for Wellington and the Hurricanes as well as the All Blacks, posted on Twitter: 'Happy belated bday to our fallen uso We love you JCTerminator.' (Uso is Samoan for brother.)

Collins made his debut for New Zealand in Christchurch in 2001 against Argentina and played fifty matches over the next seven years, forty-eight of them tests. He was regarded as one of the hardest of tacklers, as a Frenchman,

Getty

Teammates Filo Tiatia, Tana Umaga (a cousin), Ma'a Nonu and Chris Masoe were pallbearers at Jerry Collins' funeral at Porirua in June 2015.

Sebastien Chabal, might testify after a memorable hit in a test in 2007.

Collins captained the All Blacks on occasion, including one test in Argentina in 2006 when the New Zealand party was split because of a test in Auckland one week and another a week later in Buenos Aires. He impressed his hosts when he delivered a brief speech in Spanish.

Collins became something of a folk hero in Devon in 2007 when he was spotted on holiday by a Barnstaple rugby coach, who asked Collins if he'd mind running a coaching session for the local kids. He happily did so and when asked, so the story goes, how the club could repay him, he said he'd like a game. So Collins played for the Barnstaple Seconds against Newton Abbot. A few weeks later when he played for the Barbarians against South Africa, he followed tradition and wore club socks — Barnstaple club socks.

Collins wound down his career by playing in Wales, Japan and France. He was contracted to Narbonne when he died.

A MAN APART

Can there have been a rugby player who polarised opinion in New Zealand more than Sonny Bill Williams? Venerated by some, vilified by others. He had an in and out career of almost a decade with the All Blacks, and seldom was he not in the headlines, both real and metaphoric.

Sometimes he was in the news for genuine reasons, sometimes for reasons of his own manufacture. But he could not have contrived some of the unusual circumstances in which he found himself. Take the end of the 2015 World Cup final, for example. Williams was wandering around the ground with coach Steve Hansen and his teammates, thanking spectators for their support. Out from the crowd darted a small boy (Charlie Line, fourteen, as it transpired), who raced towards the All Blacks, just inside what had been the field of play. A security guard raced on and tackled him heavily and unnecessarily. Concerned All Blacks milled around; Hansen stopped to check the boy was all right. Williams moved in, put a massive arm around the boy's thin shoulders, then took his winner's medal from around his own neck and placed the ribbon over the boy's head. He then escorted young Charlie back to relatives in the lower seats of the stand. It was clear Williams told him he could keep the medal. The Twickenham lights could have been doused, the boy's face lit up so much. Four years later, after the cup playoff match, Williams gave his boots to a boy in the stand.

Controversy seemed as a moth to Williams' flame, but there was no denying the genuineness of these gestures; or the measure of his concern and distress, via social media, at the time of the March murders in Christchurch in 2019. Williams' adoption of Islam was one of the factors that stood him apart, as if his extraordinary athleticism and delicate ball skills were not enough to do that. But then Islam led him down another path of difference when he wouldn't wear a jersey with a bank logo on it; perhaps it was testament to his powers that he was the one player allowed to be different.

A superficial news media made much of Williams' appearances as a boxer, but that diversion was the least of his differences. Many All Blacks had been boxers before him, some of them very good boxers indeed — at least three, Brian McCleary, Maurice McHugh and Kevin Skinner, had been national champions.

There was talk he was lured to the game for perhaps a million; that he was really wanted for the national sevens team; that he wasn't too fussed about provincial or Super rugby — just the big show. That's the way it was with Williams; there was always talk.

THE BEST OF ALL?

There was no World Cup in 2013; it was one of those in-between years, when countries which shape their international calendars around cups shed some players from the past and look to others for the future. Yet 2013 should stand high and proud in New Zealand rugby memories.

That was the year the All Blacks became the first team to win every game

Getty

Ryan Crotty, the last-second try-scorer, Richie McCaw and Ma'a Nonu after the All Blacks beat Ireland and made it thirteen from thirteen.

in a calendar year since professionalism began in 1995. There had been smaller rugby-playing nations, which World Rugby dismisses into tiers, but none could match the All Blacks' feat of playing thirteen tests in eight different countries and winning the lot.

From Auckland to La Plata, Dunedin to Tokyo, Christchurch to Dublin, the All Blacks had an unsullied debit column. In just over five months, thirteen tests in eight different countries. And they won the lot. They played one of the leading rugby countries in the world on four occasions and won each time. Their second win against France was by 30 points to nil — it was the first time France had failed to score against New Zealand. It was probably also the first time that one of the world's leading rugby countries (the multinational Lions excepted) lost four times in one year to the one opponent.

Of countries which have won the World Cup, during 2013 the All Blacks beat Australia three times, South Africa twice and England once.

In rugby's professional era that goes back to the last quarter of 1995, none of the major rugby countries had gone through a similarly significant programme of matches in a calendar year and won them all. England have since matched the All Blacks' feat with thirteen wins from thirteen in 2016, a year in which they did not play New Zealand.

The *Guardian* newspaper in London wondered what the best sports team of all time was. One of its reporters, Tom Lutz, came up with some he felt he could mention in the same breath as the New Zealand rugby team. His first was the Spanish soccer team, which had won the last two European championships and the 2010 World Cup. But they lost to Brazil in the final of the Confederations Cup. He also mentioned the Australian league team, the United States basketball team, South Africa's cricketers and even the British cycling team though it's hardly a team sport. The Lutz list was published and readers were invited to agree (or not). A few came up with their own suggestions, such as Russian synchronised swimming, Chinese table tennis, Indonesian badminton. The All Blacks gained 61 per cent support in the very unscientific poll; next was the Spaniards, with 10 per cent.

THE MOSTLY BLACKS

In a simpler age, All Blacks jerseys were worn only by those who had earned the right to do so and the jerseys couldn't be bought in shops. Jerseys were as uncluttered as the era. Black, white collar, silver fern on the left breast.

If there were a clash of colours, the normal procedure was for the home team to change. Thus, when the All Blacks played away in Scotland or France, it was the Scots or French who changed. Sometimes the French didn't bother and no one seemed to mind. When France toured New Zealand in 1961 and 1968, no thought was given to the All Blacks wearing something different.

At that stage, they'd changed only once before. That was in 1930 when Great Britain arrived to tour with dark blue jerseys with a badge outlined in gold of three lions passant, a heraldic symbol more associated with England than with the other countries involved, Scotland, Wales and Ireland. The British manager, James ('Bim') Baxter, insisted New Zealand could not wear black and the New Zealand union chairman, Stan Dean, said Britain would have to find something else. After a few days of uncertainty, New Zealand backed down and the All Blacks wore white jerseys for the first time for the four tests. The national Maori team wore white as well for its match against Britain. By the time the next British team toured, in 1950, they'd adopted the now-familiar red jerseys so there was no clash.

It was forty-five years before the All Blacks wore white again. This was for the test in Auckland when Scotland toured for the first time and the NZRFU unhesitatingly and uncomplainingly followed the proper procedure of the home team changing.

This applied too when the All Blacks met Scotland in a World Cup quarter-final in Christchurch in 1987, even though it being a cup match, there was theoretically no home team. But rugby still followed tradition then, before rigid and inflexible cup rules were developed. When the two next met in a cup, in South Africa in 1995, New Zealand again wore white.

Thereafter, professionalism had taken hold of the game, the marketing of jerseys became big business, television had an increasing say in what teams had to do, and jersey colour decisions were made sometimes without any obvious reason. On one infamous occasion, in the World Cup in 2007, the All Blacks wore grey.

Since then, England have played in black, Wales in green, Scotland in orange . . . it's a multi-hued rugby world, but the All Blacks by and large have remained black.

TO THE POINT

Some nineteenth-century worthy was supposed to have come up with the phrase 'lies, damned lies and statistics' to illustrate how numbers can be manipulated to make a point. It could be applied in rugby to the modern mania for the array of statistics which supposedly demonstrate a team's superiority, whereas anyone in rugby knows that points on the board trump carry metres or run metres every time.

But there's one statistic in New Zealand rugby that's inviolate. That's the number of points scored by a player in a match, a season or a career. Take the All Blacks in tests, for example. Dan Carter scored 1598 points in his career, more than 600 better than the next best, the 967 scored by Andrew Mehrtens.

Ah, people might say, but Carter played in a lot more matches and therefore had many more chances to score. That's true, he did, 112 tests as a matter of fact. And that leads to a match average of nearly seventeen — itself way above Mehrtens' 13.8, itself impressive enough.

But even Carter doesn't come out on top if only match averages are calculated. That spot of honour belongs to Simon Culhane, who scored 114 in his six-match career, which gives him a staggering average of nineteen (inflated of course by his forty-five on debut against Japan in 1995). But if there's a qualification of a minimum number of matches, say ten, the method that cricket uses to calculate meaningful averages, Carter is way out in front.

Getty

Simon Culhane lines up a kick at goal in 1996.

Next on the match average basis is Grant Fox, whose 645 points came in just forty-six tests, giving him an average of fourteen. Then there's Mehrtens, then there's the only other two with an average of better than ten, Allan Hewson (201 from nineteen) and Tony Brown (171 from seventeen).

Don Clarke, the fullback for a decade from 1956 and the man they called The Boot, scored what was then a phenomenal 207 points over thirty-one matches, giving him an average of 6.6. This would be where some outraged baby boomer exclaims, 'There's lies, damned lies and statistics.' Clarke and his contemporaries and predecessors, and some of his successors, had to kick heavy leather balls that absorbed moisture so that on lousy days, of which there were many since rugby is played in the winter, they would get heavier and heavier. And grounds were wet and muddy, sometimes with the consistency (but not the taste) of porridge. Carter and his ilk, for example, had synthetic balls and played on pristine surfaces.

All of which is true.

HAVES AND HAVE-NOTS

Rugby has its 'haves' and its 'have-nots' — played a test, that is. At the end of 2019, there had been 1186 All Blacks, only 868 of whom had played in a test match. That leaves 318 who have worn the jersey, have the status-for-life of having been an All Black, but who have not played in a test match.

There are two main reasons for this divide. The first was that the first All Blacks date from 1884, but the first test match was only in 1903; All Blacks through the 1890s, therefore, and some of them remain household names, had no opportunity to play in a test match.

The other is that for so long in rugby history, it was the outer rugby countries such as New Zealand, Australia and South Africa which toured, not the individual British and Irish countries. They didn't tour on the basis that they were represented, or supposed to be, in the various combined sides which are now known retrospectively as the British and Irish Lions. The effect was that a New Zealander could go on a long tour, play many games for his country, but not play a test. Only in the 1960s and 70s when the individual British countries started touring could that also apply to them.

Statistics could be a cruel judge. Frank Wilson was an All Black who played twice for New Zealand in 1910. He was killed in the Battle of the Somme in 1916, but because he hadn't played a test, he was not included in some northern hemisphere lists of rugby internationals who died in war.

Bevan Holmes, a useful No. 8 and flanker from Northland, has the distinction of playing most games for the All Blacks without playing a test. He went on the long tours of South Africa and the northern hemisphere in 1970 and 1972–73, as well as playing on an internal tour, and played thirty-one times.

Six others played more than twenty tour matches without a test, while the list also includes some distinguished players, including Alf Bayly in the nineteenth century and Graeme Crossman in the twentieth who both captained the All Blacks. The list also includes one of the most noted coaches in the rugby world, Warren Gatland.

The top few:
Bevan Holmes (1970, 72–73) 31
Kevin Barry (1962–64) 23
Lin Colling (1972–73) 21
Keith Bagley (1953–54) 20
Handley Brown (1924–26) 20
William McKenzie (1893–94, 96–97) 20
Fred Murray (1893, 97) 20
Alf Bayly (1893–94, 97) 19
Graeme Crossman (1974, 76) 19
Ian Eliason (1972–73) 19
Warren Gatland (1988–91) 17
Cyril Pepper (1935–36) 17

REMEMBERING WINS

On the French celebration day of the year, Bastille Day (14 July) in 2019, some ageing rugby stars got together again for some celebrating of their own. Forty years before, at Eden Park in Auckland, they'd beaten New Zealand 24–19. Not only was it the first French away win against the All Blacks, it was also on France's day of days. In the words of their national anthem which rang out again and again that night, '*le jour de gloire est arrivé!*'

The halfback Jérôme Gallion, not wanted for the first test which New Zealand won 23–9, but who regained his spot for Auckland, laughingly recalled at the reunion that those not chosen for the second test were considered lucky because the pre-match fear was that the All Blacks would win by even more. Gallion became one of the 'unlucky' ones and played.

Their big blindside flanker, Jean-Luc Joinel, carrying his years as well as he carried the ball in his salad days, laughed at the memories. The partying in Auckland went on well into the night and they left for Tahiti the next day. Joinel remembered the players' joy as they crossed the international dateline and realised they would have another Bastille Day in Papeete.

A few months after the French reunion, similarly ageing Englishmen gathered in the tiny West Yorkshire market town of Otley, about 15 km from Leeds, there to celebrate their own victory against the All Blacks, the time the Northern Division (as it was then called) won 21–9. The North were captained that day by Billy Beaumont, the lock who also captained England and who went on to be chairman of World Rugby; he had with him six other members of the England team that played the All Blacks on the following Saturday. But what the North did at Otley, England failed to do at Twickenham.

It's a sort of compliment to the All Blacks that teams which beat them celebrate long into their lifetimes; a win against New Zealand is given more significance than wins against anyone else, it seems. Especially in Wales, teams love beating the All Blacks and love almost as much talking and singing about it for years to come. Swansea, Cardiff, Newport and Llanelli all made a happy point of remembering some of their most celebrated days in rugby. And the Welsh union itself gave a nod to the winning history when it decided each of the four would be New Zealand's opponents on the Welsh centenary tour in 1980.

SCHOOLS' CUP

The Moascar Cup began its rugby life in New Zealand after the First World War as a Ranfurly Shield for school First XVs — a challenge trophy for the best of school teams.

But the real challenge has been how to keep the cup relevant and for it to be worthy of a prize sought by schoolboys.

The cup, as the name implies, had its beginning in Egypt. British, New Zealand and Australian soldiers camped at Moascar in Ismailia at the northern end of the Suez Canal, east of Cairo, formed the Ismailia Rugby Union and organised a rugby competition. The Ismailia Rugby Union then organised a cup — described as 'a handsome Irish cup' — and had it mounted on a piece of a wooden propeller from a German aircraft shot down in Palestine. Thus, the Moascar Cup came into being and was won by the New Zealand Mounted Rifles Unit and Depot, which won nine of its ten matches.

'The contest assumed an international aspect both because of the personnel of the teams and the high standard of play attained,' one who was there wrote. The cup was brought home and presented to the NZRFU on condition that it be a challenge trophy for secondary schools.

The two schools to play for it the first time — Christchurch Boys' High School and Palmerston North BHS — were selected, based on their record in recent years. They met for the cup at Athletic Park in Wellington in 1920 in appalling conditions. Prime Minister William Massey and several cabinet ministers, having adjourned Parliament for the afternoon, 'sat miserably' in the main grandstand. There was no score at the end of normal time so extra time was played and the referee ruled that if there was still no score, 'force-downs' (i.e. a touchdown in goal) would count. A Palmerston North player kicked the

Willie Ripia, captain of the Rotorua Boys' High School First XV, holds aloft the Moascar Cup after beating Napier Boys' High School. Ripia went on to play for New Zealand Maori, the Highlanders and the Hurricanes.

ball dead and that was deemed a force-down. Christchurch BHS thus became the first holders.

But as the years unwound, some schools came to believe that the cup placed too much emphasis on winning and others that schools such as Te Aute had an unfair advantage because it had boys, so it was said, who matured earlier than Pakeha boys.

There were long periods when there were no cup matches at all, but it gained something of a second wind thanks to an enthusiastic Wellington reporter, Arthur Reeve. 'During my years of reporting on college rugby, I made it my business to revive and promote Moascar Cup games,' he wrote.

Even so, there are still some rugby schools — Otago and Southland Boys' High Schools, Christ's College, Westlake BHS, among others — which have yet to win it.

THORN IN THE SIDE

He turned down the chance to be an All Black one year, saved the All Blacks from losing a test in another, and he helped win the World Cup in yet another. That's Brad Thorn.

And that's only one half of the sporting life of Bradley Carnegie Thorn, who also played league for Australia under two organisations (Super League and the NRL), for Queensland in state of origin and won premierships with the Brisbane Broncos.

Thorn, who'd moved to Australia from Dunedin with his family when young, had always had an affinity with the All Blacks when growing up and forging his league career. Towards the end of 2000, when he was twenty-five, he moved to Christchurch to try to make his rugby mark. Robbie Deans put him in the Crusaders and he played eleven games as a No. 8 or flanker.

Steve Hansen was then coaching Canterbury and he moved Thorn to lock; he played in fifteen matches that year, including going on as a substitute in the successful final against Otago. This was the year in which the All Blacks coach, Wayne Smith, said he didn't know if he wanted the job and the New Zealand union went through a hurried process of interviews and appointed John Mitchell.

Deans became Mitchell's 'coaching co-ordinator' and when their squad for matches in the northern hemisphere was named, Thorn was in it. But not for long. Thorn told the manager, Andrew Martin, that he didn't know if he was committed to rugby and that he might go back to league.

He took a year off and returned to the Crusaders in 2003, made such an impression that Mitchell chose him again and he made his delayed debut in Hamilton against Wales. He played in all seven matches in the World Cup, then went back to league.

Thorn returned to rugby again in 2008 and became an integral member of the New Zealand pack for the next three years. It was during this stint that he brought off a stunning tackle that stopped a try and probably an All Blacks loss. In Wellington in 2009, French wing Vincent Clerc was haring

Brad Thorn during one of the All Blacks' celebration parades in 2011.

for the goal-line and a try seemed inevitable until out of the night emerged the charging figure of Thorn who brought him down. A bunch of former All Blacks sitting together in the back of the stand rose as one. They knew the significance.

Thorn's unusual All Blacks career ended with success in the 2011 World Cup final.

BLACK NIGHT

It used to be an article of rugby faith that matches between New Zealand and South Africa were tense encounters, little between the two teams and any mistake would signal a win for one and a loss for the other.

Even though the All Blacks got away on the Springboks in the win-loss stakes in the professional era, their meetings were still seen as the tectonic plates of the game grinding away.

Until Albany Stadium on Auckland's North Shore on 16 September 2017. On that night, the ninety-fourth test between the two countries, New Zealand humiliated South Africa 57–0, reducing a rugby country with a proud record to a state of bewilderment. It was South Africa's biggest loss in 126 years of playing test rugby. The All Blacks had prevented the Springboks from scoring before, but never with a margin like this.

It was one of those nights on which the All Blacks thrived on confidence and on which the Springboks wondered what on earth they could do. Everything went right for the All Blacks, nothing for the Springboks.

The deluge began after a quarter of an hour when halfback Aaron Smith took a tap penalty from around halfway, kicked (unusually) with his left foot and the ball bounced sweetly up in front of wing Rieko Ioane. It's when moves like that come off that teams collectively think it's their night so they try more. Like Beauden Barrett twenty metres out from the line, Springboks to the left of him and Springboks to the right of him, flipping the ball audaciously and one-handed back to Nehe Milner-Skudder who scored one of his two tries for the night.

As always, the forwards provided the stability and the momentum to allow the backs to pull off their fancy moves; they also provided a defence that was unbending in the face of some determined South African attacking that eventually, accepting the inevitable, faded away to not much.

Captain Kieran Read tried to be charitable towards the Springboks after the game, but he left with one of the great understatements: 'The scoreline probably didn't look pretty for them . . .'

South Africans may have felt, with some justification, that this was the nadir of their rugby. But three weeks later, with New Zealand fielding the same team — except for Scott Barrett in place of Brodie Retallick — it was like it always used to be (or seemed like it always used to be). At Newlands in Cape Town, the All Blacks won by just a point against a changed Springbok team but which still had nine starters from the Albany anguish.

RUGBY GREATNESS

There are different ways to measure greatness. By the use of statistics; by subjective or objective comparison with others; by extremely unscientific straw polls; by the acclamation of others.

Whatever method is used, Colin Meads had greatness in rugby. In his youth and playing pomp, he had ability and authority on the field; teammates revered him and opponents respected him. In his later life, whether working for the intellectually handicapped in King Country, making endless after-dinner speeches that packed in crowds even though they'd heard it all before, or just leaning quietly on a bar, pint glass lost in one massive hand, Meads was a magnet.

A rugby magazine voted him player of the century at the end of the twentieth century; many of those who voted probably never saw him play because he'd stopped nearly thirty years before, but that didn't seem to matter.

When the All Blacks were in South Africa for the World Cup in 1995, the players included some of the finest the game has seen — Jonah Lomu, Jeff

Getty

SIR COLIN MEADS
ALL BLACK
1957–1971
New Zealand's Player
of the 20th Century

Colin Meads and wife Verna by his statue the day it was unveiled. He died two months later.

Wilson, Sean Fitzpatrick — but Meads as the manager was still an attraction.

A Scottish journalist of considerable ability but more known for writing about soccer and boxing, Hugh McIlvanney, was there and wrote that if one man embodied all the respect and apprehension and downright awe that are stirred by the mention of the All Blacks' name, that man was surely Meads.

'From the day he made his international debut, in 1957 against Australia, he was a force in global rugby the like of which it may never see again,' McIlvanney wrote. 'Force is the appropriate term for Meads was the ultimate hard man's hard man . . . his was the kind of combativeness that is never out of date.'

His audiences in his rugby after-life loved his homespun tales; it was rugby in the rough. Like when he hit Welshman Jeff Young for being on the All Blacks' side of the lineout once too often: 'I was sorry I broke his jaw, but I wasn't sorry I hit him.' And when referee Pat Murphy penalised Young rather than Meads: 'Now, that's what I call a good referee.'

When a statue of Meads was unveiled in Te Kuiti, it was one of the town's biggest days. Another big day was not long after when Meads died and his funeral service was telecast and streamed live. The Prime Minister was there. The Leader of the Opposition was there. That's another measure of greatness.

It was the first time that had happened. The next time was for the funeral of Meads' great mate, Sir Brian Lochore.

COACHING CHANGES

One of the enduring characteristics of the modern era of rugby is not so much the longevity of players, although that has been greatly extended, but of coaches.

A man revered as one of the best coaches the All Blacks have had, Fred Allen, coached in just fourteen test matches for a perfect record. Another of high standing, Brian Lochore, was coach in just eighteen matches. Some coaches well known in their time, Bob Duff in the early seventies and Eric Watson in 1979–80, didn't even get into double figures for test matches.

Getty

Steve Hansen

But the two dominant coaches of the twenty-first century, Steve Hansen and Graham Henry, are Methuselahs in test terms compared with the others. Henry took over from John Mitchell (twenty-eight tests) in 2004 and when he stepped down after the 2011 World Cup, he'd coached the All Blacks in 103 test matches, with a highly respectable record of eighty-eight wins and fifteen losses for a career percentage of 85.4.

His assistant for much of that time, Steve Hansen, then took over and by the time he quit in 2019 for a quieter life in Japan, he'd coached the All Blacks in 107 test matches for ninety-three wins, four draws and ten losses for an 86.9 per cent record.

Some of their predecessors wouldn't have even seen that many test matches in their lifetimes.

Coaching as a fulltime, well-paid job is one of the factors that kept Henry and Hansen there for so long (success also being a factor in their retention). But they also had administrative and coaching support of a level that some of their predecessors couldn't imagine.

Take the first All Blacks coach, Jimmy Duncan. He'd been captain in New Zealand's first test in 1903 at the age of thirty-three, then coach in the first test in New Zealand the following year, at the age of thirty-four. The year after that, he marked his thirty-fifth birthday in London during the 1905–06 team's tour. Accounts differ, but one recollection was that he didn't really coach those All Blacks because two players, Bill Cunningham in the forwards and Billy Stead with the backs, took over. Nevertheless, Duncan was the official coach for the six months or so the team was away.

For a time, the All Blacks never had a coach at all because the practice was frowned upon by the self-appointed guardians of the game, the English union. For many years, the position of coach was hidden under the title of assistant manager.

DIFFERENT COUNTING

Under current arrangements and assuming there's no change — and that's always a possibility — Australia will mark their 200th test against New Zealand in 2022. But New Zealand won't. New Zealand will have to wait another twenty-four tests before it can mark 200 matches against their oldest opponents.

The discrepancy is in the counting and dates from the 1920s. That was when rugby had just about disappeared in Queensland, there was no Australian Rugby Union, and New South Wales carried the flag. New South Wales, or the Waratahs as they were sometimes (but not always) known, played in their own name but also in lieu of any Australian team.

In 1987, the Australian Rugby Union decided that matches the Waratahs played on a celebrated northern hemisphere tour in 1927–28 against the 'home' countries and France deserved to be counted as full tests. So tests they became, sixty years after the event.

A Sydney chronicler of sporting doings, Jack Pollard, thought that retrospective judgement should be applied to all New South Wales matches in the twenties, and he lobbied the Australian union. The union's executive committee in July 1988 half agreed with him. Bob Fordham, the union's executive director, wrote to Pollard: 'It was resolved that during the said period when New South Wales played matches in Australia, test status would not be awarded. However, when New South Wales teams toured overseas during this period, it would be regarded that New South Wales players were in fact representing Australia and test status would be recognised.'

Pollard was persistent and eventually got his way for all matches to be tests. Sometimes NSW matches in New Zealand in the 1920s were described as tests and players were awarded caps. But the New Zealand union has never followed the Australian lead, partly because there were too many inconsistencies. On occasions, the New Zealand team playing New South Wales was a third- or even fourth-string All Blacks team; the selectors used the state games as trials on occasions and had different policies at different times. In 1925, for example, members of the returning Invincibles from Britain were declared ineligible to go to New South Wales with an All Blacks team, but later in the year New Zealand played New South Wales in Auckland and the All Blacks were almost entirely Invincibles.

The Australian retrospective decision also implied that Victoria during the 1920s did not count as a rugby state. But the Victorian union continued to exist and, towards the end of the decade, provided at least two Wallabies.

A TRIBAL SPORT

Rugby is a tribal sport. Followers have a passionate allegiance at different levels of the game — school, club, province, Super Rugby and, ultimately, the national team. For many people, the loyalties stay with them, no matter how far removed they physically may be from school, club, province or country.

They take pride especially in how many All Blacks may have been produced from 'their' area, even though it's mostly a numbers game. It's logical that most All Blacks come from the more populous areas so without getting into a thorny discussion about actual numbers, it's obvious that the provinces which have produced most All Blacks have been Auckland, Canterbury, Wellington and Otago.

Schools are the most reliable measure of where All Blacks come from because all future All Blacks at some stage went to school and, from early in the twentieth century, most went to a secondary school. Again, it's a numbers game. At the end of 2019, Auckland Grammar had the most All Blacks with fifty-three, followed by Christchurch Boys' High School with forty-four and Wellington College, thirty-one.

All Blacks' clubs too are easy enough to calculate if a simple yardstick is used: a player must have been playing with a club when chosen for New Zealand for that club to be able to claim him as an All Black. The two outstanding clubs are Ponsonby in Auckland, which can claim forty-seven All Blacks, and the University club in Dunedin, which has produced forty-five. Each club can claim many more who had been All Blacks before they joined their clubs or who became All Blacks later, but they are All Blacks of other clubs. Ponsonby can also claim players for other test-playing countries, especially Samoa, Tonga and Fiji.

Schools, clubs and provinces also avidly count, and take pride in, those of their players who go on to the national women's team, the Black Ferns.

Counting has been coloured in the professional era by All Blacks seldom appearing in provincial matches and hardly at all in club matches. There was a time when players might play a test on a Saturday, then for their provincial side or their club on the next day. That changed when players went on the payroll and now an All Blacks coach will 'release' players he doesn't immediately need. As the paymaster, the New Zealand union through its coach can also determine whether players should play for a Super Rugby side. This applies especially in World Cup years when players seen to be of likely importance in the cup campaign are nursed through the preceding months.

AT THE DOUBLE

Plenty of rugby players have been good at other sports; it goes almost without saying that if players are particularly good at one sport, chances are they'll be pretty good at another. At the highest level, many All Blacks have played at a national level in another sport.

But there's a special cachet for those who have played for their country at rugby and at cricket: the double All Blacks, as they've been known. Setting them apart — and there's not many — was probably because for much of the twentieth century, the seasons were distinct and rugby was the main winter sport and cricket in summer. That's changed with professionalism in rugby and the rise in participation in, and popularity of, other sports. Seasons are blurred almost to the point of obliteration and specialisation in a modern era has ruled out diversity.

There have been seven 'double All Blacks' — George Dickinson the first in the 1920s, then Charlie Oliver, Curly Page, Eric Tindill and Bill Carson before the Second World War, and only two since, Brian McKechnie in the late 1970s and early 1980s and Jeff Wilson in the late twentieth and early twenty-first centuries.

Of those, Tindill alone played both test cricket and test rugby. He played four cricket tests against England and one against Australia before and after the Second World War. His sole rugby test was against England in the 'Obolensky match' at Twickenham in 1936. He twice toured Australia with the cricketers and once with the All Blacks. He also had a hand in the dismissal of Don Bradman for eleven in the only match Bradman played against New Zealand. That was in Adelaide in 1937 when the cricketers were on the way home by ship from their tour of England. As wicketkeeper, Tindill caught Bradman off the bowling of Jack Cowie.

If that wasn't enough for Tindill, he also refereed rugby tests (two against the British Isles in 1950) and umpired cricket tests.

There's a diversity of excellence apart from cricket by other All Blacks. Among them: George Smith, a member of the 1905–06 team, was a hurdler good enough to win national titles in New Zealand and England and set an unofficial world record. Many others won national athletics titles, including Peter Henderson who ran in the final of the 100 yards at the Empire Games in Auckland in 1950. Gary Knight was a wrestling bronze medallist at the Commonwealth Games in 1974; Ron Jarden competed in Admiral's Cup yachting; Andy Leslie and Bill Davis played softball for New Zealand; several All Blacks won national boxing titles and latterly, there's been the one-of-a-kind Sonny Bill Williams.

Getty

Jeff Wilson playing for New Zealand in 2005, his last year of top-level cricket.

CAPPING IT OFF

Caps are one of rugby's oldest traditions, begun at the English public school that gave the game its name.

Velvet caps were introduced in the 1830s to be worn by those boys senior enough to 'play up' in the main body of the match; the caps were eminently more suitable and rugged than the top hats the boys previously wore. From then, the caps followed the game's development as a mark of distinction.

Caps had a place in the earliest days of New Zealand rugby, sometimes awarded by clubs but more often by provincial unions. Photos of the first New Zealand team in 1884 show players wearing their provincial caps and not, as is sometimes thought, New Zealand caps. That team came eight years before the formation of the New Zealand union and had no official status until the

A New Zealand Natives cap from the 1888–89 tour.

1920s when the NZRFU made a retrospective judgement and decided each surviving player should be awarded a cap. (An 1884 cap that sold for several thousand dollars at auction in recent years was in fact one of those 1920s caps, not from 1884.)

The Natives of 1888–89, also a private venture team, had caps made, and the awarding of caps became routine once the NZRFU took over. For an unrecorded reason, most likely cost, the practice lapsed in the 1930s, although there's confusion about precisely when. Charlie Saxton, an All Black in 1938, said he never received a cap; Ron Ward of Southland, an All Black in 1936, did receive a cap but Jack Rankin, also a 1936 All Black, did not.

The next New Zealand caps to be awarded were when the World Cup began in New Zealand in 1987. Each member of the winning New Zealand squad was given a cap at a farewell dinner the night after the final.

But then the practice lapsed again until well into the professional era and the New Zealand union, when Jock Hobbs was chairman, started holding capping ceremonies around the country for All Blacks of past years who had never received the physical cap. Many of the older players were visibly moved to be so honoured so long after they'd played the game.

The very word 'cap' came to be used as a verb as well as a noun: players gaining international status are said to be capped and the word even has been applied to selection in teams below national status. The word also is used to indicate whether an international match is of full test status; for example, whether it's a 'cap match' or whether it's a 'non-cap test'.

NOT QUITE ALL BLACKS

When Liam Squire made himself unavailable for the All Blacks in 2019, there were questions about how many other players have turned down the chance to play for New Zealand, or been chosen then not played.

The answer was plenty, for many different reasons.

The first was George Campbell, who was wanted to lead the first New

Zealand team, to New South Wales in 1884; he turned the chance down because of work, a decision he regretted for the rest of his life. (Campbell worked for the government's audit department. Forty years later, he was Arthur Carman's boss in 1924 when Carman asked for leave to go to Britain as a journalist with the All Blacks; Campbell told Carman it was too good a chance to turn down.)

One of the cruellest cases of a player being picked to play for the All Blacks, then not doing so, was in 1921. Henry Mullins, a Canterbury halfback, was chosen one week by the three New Zealand selectors for the All Blacks team to play New South Wales in Christchurch. On virtually the eve of the match a week later, Mullins was told he wasn't playing after all and that Teddy Roberts was on his way down from Wellington. Needless to say, that incensed Canterbury people and mystified the rest of the country.

No explanation was ever given by either the selectors or the NZRFU. Not surprisingly, Mullins switched to league and played a test against Great Britain in 1924. The selectors' vacillation came at a price: New South Wales won the match 17–0, one of New Zealand's heaviest defeats. (It was a second New Zealand team because the first was playing South Africa, but it was picked as New Zealand, nevertheless. The game was one of those deemed retrospectively by the Australian Rugby Union in the 1980s to be a test match.)

In more recent times, David Halligan was picked to play for the All Blacks against Scotland in 1981 but was injured two days before the match, withdrew and was never picked again. In the same category, a Taranaki flanker, Ross Fraser, was chosen to play for New Zealand against Argentina in 1979 but had a leg broken in a club match on the day of his selection.

There have been several cases of players, perfectly fit, turning down the chance to play for New Zealand. One was Greg Denholm, an Auckland prop, who twice during the 1970s opted for work ahead of play.

And there were the many players chosen as reserves who wore the jersey, had their photos taken in an All Blacks team, but never got on to the field.

END OF THE ROAD

When the All Blacks sorted themselves into their choreographed positions for the haka before the World Cup semifinal in Yokohama in October 2019, England's players had a formation of their own. They formed themselves into a deep V, a couple of them getting so excited they crossed the 10-metre line, the haka demarcation line as decreed by World Rugby.

In the valley of the V, with a knowing smile, was the captain Owen Farrell. But what did he know? That the French had formed up in a similar manner before the 2011 final, symbolising V for victory? But it was not a victory for France on that day.

Eight years later, the psychological game worked. Regardless of the 19–7 score, it was a comprehensive defeat for New Zealand, the team that was everyone's favourite to win the cup for a third successive time. It was a sad last farewell for players such as the captain, Kieran Read, and the wing-fullback, Ben Smith, and others, and the coach, Steve Hansen.

So unexpected was England's control that some television commentators, even with ten or fifteen minutes to go, still expressed a belief that the All Blacks could do something to lift themselves from the bog. But it had taken them

V for victory . . . England confront the haka in Yokohama.

fifty-six minutes to score, benefiting from an overthrown England lineout, whereas England had built a commanding lead even allowing for two tries that had been ruled out.

Others thought back to Perth only a couple of months before when Australia did to New Zealand what England did in Yokohama. And even the match before that, in Wellington, a test match was drawn that the South Africans could so easily have won. So the signs were there.

It was the end of the road for the All Blacks of 2019. Yes, they had an unnecessary playoff game to win (which they did), but that's like rowers competing in a B final. It's not quite the same thing.

But a curious thing happened. When the All Blacks had failed in their cup quests before, especially in 1999 and 2003, bitter recriminations followed. Coaches were publicly reviled and replaced, one was spat at as if he were a failed politician in a banana republic. The national mood was ugly.

This time, the loss seemed to be accepted with a collective shrug. It helped that Hansen and Read were gracious losers (in public anyway), it helped that the England coach, Eddie Jones, didn't crow (as New Zealanders knew he could). Some talked about a new national maturity. More likely, thanks to 2011 and 2015, the desperate longing to win the cup had been satisfied.

FINDING THE GOAT

Americans have given the world new words, new meanings of old words and an alphabet soup of acronyms.

One of the last is GOAT. The word's use in sport, especially in the United States, used to apply in a derogatory sense — someone who lost a game for a team was a goat. But by the 1990s it had turned into an acronym and the first use, apparently, applied to Muhammad Ali. His wife, Lonnie, in 1992 registered a company, Greatest Of All Time Inc, which became GOAT.

Social media got hold of it and it's now commonplace when assessing someone or something's worth or comparing someone or something with others.

Richie McCaw with the World Cup in 2011 . . . the GOAT?

So who is the GOAT of New Zealand rugby? Any answer is of course subjective, someone's GOAT could be someone else's cart-horse. Across the great span of rugby of 150 years, the game has changed enormously and therefore players' roles have changed. It's not possible to validly compare Billy Wallace, for example, with Jeff Wilson or with Ben Smith; the only similarities are that all played rugby for New Zealand at wing or fullback.

When Colin Meads was voted by a magazine to be its player of the twentieth century, Meads himself was one of several to point out that Maurice Brownlie, for example, had the standing in his day that Meads had in his. Or Charlie Seeling a generation earlier, or Brodie Retallick a couple of generations later.

A superficial judgement would favour those who score points because it's points that win matches, but points-scorers have to benefit from the efforts of their teammates. Even a rare phenomenon such as Jonah Lomu had to get the ball from someone. Rugby in many ways is the ultimate team game: the whole utilising and benefiting from each one of its constituent parts.

It's necessary when ascribing greatness to go beyond the game, to examine more than just a player's impact. Brian Lochore, for example, graced the game and had admirable qualities beyond it. There was talk at his funeral among some who knew him well that he would have been the ideal governor-general: a friend to all, a harsh word about few, and most of all, no harsh words about him.

Richie McCaw of modern players would come closest to being the GOAT. If one game of his many stood out as an example of his commitment to his cause and his capacity for work, it was the World Cup final of 2011. New Zealand surely would have lost that final without him.

So the GOAT? Make up your own mind.

ACKNOWLEDGEMENTS

To all with some role in the game, then or now, player, administrator, referee, St John people, journalist, author, historian, to all of them, Ron Palenski gives thanks. Without interest in the game, it would have withered and died ages ago, perhaps reduced to a minor sport played by just a few aficionados. There's particular gratitude for those who have recorded their thoughts and deeds, or had them recorded for them, whether in books, newspapers, magazines or, increasingly, online. The digital era has made the past accessible like never before; let's hope the present becomes just as accessible for those in the future. A particular thanks to John Griffiths in the United Kingdom and Robert Messenger and Steve Johnson in Australia, and to the many in New Zealand who record rugby's minutiae for the benefit of us all. Thanks also to Kevin Chapman and Warren Adler from Upstart and, as always, Kathy.